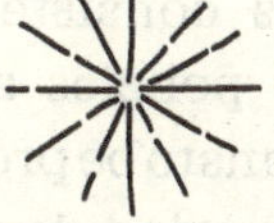

We (Still) Be Lovin' Black Children:
African Diaspora Literacy, A Divine Ancestral Charge

The title, *We (Still) Be Lovin' Black Children*, establishes its premise. 'Be Lovin' connotes an immediacy, a now-ness, a persistence that is culturally based and applicable to today's enigmatic conditions. Give every new African and African American mother a copy of *We (Still) Be Lovin' Black Children* and the intricate, complex maze through which she must meander in her quest for emotional freedom is diminished. *We (Still) Be Lovin' Black Children* means we have been, are now, and will be lovin' and minimizing the barriers that separate us. It is explicit and replete with examples of the *how*. With the wisdom of loving scholars and teachers, the chains of oppression are weakened and eventually severed.

**Dr. Adelaide L. Sanford, Vice-Chancellor Emerita,
New York State Board of Regents**

Black parents can no longer settle for 'the Talk' as a defense for our children. They need information, strategies, and tactics for ensuring Black children survive AND thrive in an increasingly hostile world. *We (Still) Be Lovin' Black Children* is the corrective our families need to raise the mentally, emotionally, socially, and culturally healthy children we need to ensure the legacies left over the millennia and throughout the world.

**Dr. Gloria Ladson-Billings
Professor Emerita and the former Kellner Family
Distinguished Professor at the University of
Wisconsin-Madison, past President of the American
Educational Research Association (AERA)**

As educational systems consistently demonstrate anti-Blackness through their policies and practices, this book shows readers what it means to be pro-Black and consequently pro-Black children. By tearing down divisive barriers and unnecessary borders, the book exemplifies what is possible in a global movement dedicated to Blackness in the fight for racial justice! This book teaches as it troubles racial injustices everywhere!

Dr. H. Richard Milner IV
Cornelius Vanderbilt Chair of Education,
Vanderbilt University

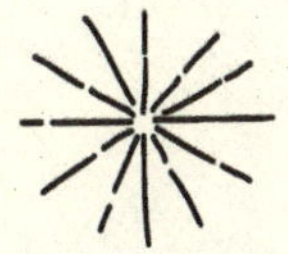

We (Still) Be Lovin' Black Children

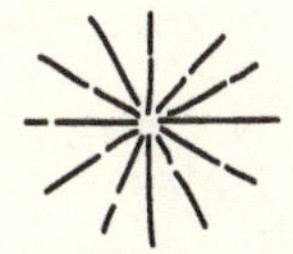

We (Still) Be Lovin' Black Children

African Diaspora Literacy, A Divine Ancestral Charge, 2nd Edition

EDITED BY
GLORIA SWINDLER BOUTTE,
JOYCE E. KING,
GEORGE L. JOHNSON, JR.,
LaGARRETT J. KING,
AND JARVAIS J. JACKSON

GORHAM, MAINE

 # Contents

CONTENTS

Acknowledgments

We extend gratitude to our ancestors, family members, friends, and loved ones who made this work possible. Special thanks are extended to the magnificent Dr. (Nana) Joyce E. King, who introduced the concept of diaspora literacy and inspired generations of scholar-activists—some of whom contributed to this work and scores of unnamed mentees and admirers. As usual, Jarvais Jackson, University of South Carolina doctoral student, willingly shared his artistic talents not only to design the conference booklet but also the cover of this book. Thanks to Angela Hill, doctoral student at the University of South Carolina, for her editorial assistance.

This book is the product of a small conference funded by the Spencer Foundation, which focused on African Diaspora Literacy in September 2019. Thanks to program officers, reviewers, and others who saw the promise in the grant proposal. We hope that this book makes you proud. We acknowledge the following conference attendees and extend deep appreciation for thinking together about how to better love Black children.

Janice Baines	Gloria Swindler Boutte
Anthony Broughton	Michelle Bryan
Saudah Collins	Justus Cox
Julia Dawson	Gwenda Green
Angela Hill	Kayla Hostetler
Joy Howard	Derrick Jackson
Jarvais Jackson	Tambra Jackson
Toby Jenkins	George L. Johnson, Jr.

Joyce E. King

LaGarrett King

Clement Lambert

Hassimi Maiga

Meir Muller

Susi Long

Kindel Nash

Mopelola Omoegun

Asangha Muki

Samuel Ntewesu

Nancy Tolson

Berte Van Wyk

Kamania Wynter-Hoyte

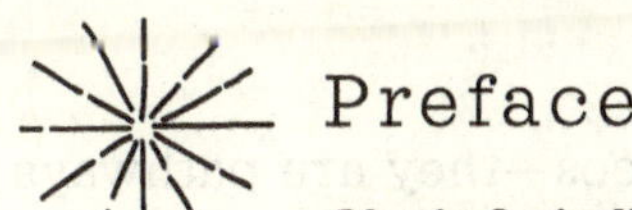

Preface

Gloria Swindler Boutte, Joyce E. King,
George L. Johnson, Jr., LaGarrett J. King,
and Jarvais J. Jackson

This second edition of *We Be Lovin' Black Children* brings together treasured chapters from the first edition alongside powerful new contributions. While youth voices were represented in the original collection, this edition deepens that commitment by featuring a full chapter authored by youth themselves, as well as introducing a new program for Black high schoolers in England.

Contributors to this volume come from the U.S. and across the globe, each with a strong record of ensuring that Black children are cherished in liberatory and life-affirming ways. To further support families, educators, and communities, we have also updated and expanded resources that nurture the ongoing work of loving Black children unapologetically and expansively.

We begin this edition with an updated Chapter 1, *Open Love Letter to Black Families and Communities*, affirming that Black culture and history have always been essential and foundational. This chapter illuminates why they remain vital—across time and space, across social status and circumstance, and across every dimension of our collective lives.

A brand-new addition, Chapter 2, *Pro-Blackness: What It Looks Like and What It Is*, brings Pro-Blackness to life. It breaks down not only what Pro-Blackness means, but also how to recognize it when you see it, how to feel it moving through you, and how to live it boldly in everyday ways.

Chapter 3, *We Be Lovin' Black History: Eight Best Teaching Practices Around Black History Education*, lifts up eight powerful principles of Black Historical Consciousness. These principles are not just best practices—they are pathways for teaching Black history with truth, depth, and a love that affirms the brilliance of Black people across time and place.

In Chapter 4, *My Soul Looks Back in Wonder: What Are We Doing to "Serve the Present Age"?*, Dr. Joyce King charges us to draw from African spiritual power and ancestral wisdom—our "weapons of the soul"—to educate and protect Black children in an era of censorship and cultural warfare. Highlighting Afrocentric initiatives in Florida, California, New York, Brazil, and Canada, she shows how truth, healing, and solidarity remain essential to serving the present age.

Chapter 5, *What the Children We Be Lovin' Have to Say*, amplifies the voices of Preston King, Jaliyah Ware, and Janiyah Ware, reminding us that Black children's words matter. Their reflections reveal both the pain of anti-Black violence and the sustaining power of Black love, resilience, and resistance. In honoring their voices, we are called to create spaces of safety and to act alongside children as they transform pain into power.

In Chapter 6, *Say It Loud—I'm Black and I'm Proud: Beauty, Brilliance, and Belonging in Our Homes, Classrooms, and Communities*, four outstanding elementary teachers share examples of family- and community-based activities that ensure children are culturally grounded.

Written by three exemplary middle school teachers, Chapter 7, *Great Rising: Activities to Inspire Black Teens and Youth*, engages readers with insights on "Black girl magic," culturally relevant approaches for teaching Black boys, and strategies to inspire all Black youth.

Chapter 8, *Preparing Black Children to Identify and Confront Racism in Books, Media, and Other Texts: Critical Questions*, written by a Jewish professor, emphasizes the power of books and other media. It provides strategies for teaching Black children to critically analyze texts—from music and television to classroom literature—through an anti-racist lens.

Chapter 9, *Each One, Teach One: Reflections and Lessons on Mentoring Young Men of Color*, offers practical mentoring advice for boys (and girls). Written by two professors—one white and one Black—it extends an invitation for all of us to take responsibility for the success of Black children and youth.

Chapter 10, *We Be Family*, is co-narrated by a white teacher and her former African American student. Together, they model what welcoming classroom "families" can look like. Jamon, the student, powerfully recalls the Black love he felt in Mrs. Hostetler's classroom and the trauma of Black history's omission in most of his schooling—except for superficial lessons on slavery and the Civil Rights Movement.

Chapter 11, *The Crown on Your Head: Teaching African Diaspora Literacy Through Hair*, is co-authored by an African American elementary teacher and her white doctoral advisor. Shayla, the teacher, shares her journey of learning to love her natural hair and offers strategies for teaching children to embrace the beauty of Black hair from an early age.

Chapter 12, *Teaching Our Children About Blackness in the World*, written by three professors, highlights Freedom Schools and Elev8te as exemplary models for cultivating global literacy. The emphasis is on nurturing critical consciousness about Blackness across the African Diaspora.

Chapter 13, *African Diaspora Literacy in Jamaica and the Wider Caribbean*, written by a professor, offers a nuanced analysis of color-consciousness and examines the impact of European educational systems on Caribbean identities.

Chapter 14, *Lessons From Africa*, authored by three African professors—Cameroonian, Ghanaian, and South African—shares timeless proverbs, stories, and cultural lessons. These foundational values provide essential wisdom for the survival and flourishing of Black children and youth.

In Chapter 15, *We Be Schoolin'. We Be Schooled: Learning Across Educator Partnerships with Youth Voices at the Center*, four authors in the United Kingdom reflecxt on B-HUGs (Black Heritage University Groups), a partnership between university faculty and high school staff in South West England dedicated to centering Black youths' voices in predominantly white schools. Through art workshops, electives, reciprocal learning, and community events, the authors show how joy, belonging, and cultural pride become essential tools for critical consciousness and educational equity.

Chapter 16, *Resources*, features a collection of new and updated resources designed to strengthen the work of families, educators, and communities committed to loving Black children. It underscores the urgency of deeply loving Black children and youth by equipping them with knowledge of African Diasporic history and culture.

As Dr. Joyce King's chapter reminds us, collectively, we have a *divine charge to keep* on behalf of Black children everywhere. At the heart of this work is an unshakable love for Black children and a commitment to ensuring that they are seen, heard, and cherished in every space. This preface closes with a call to embrace African Diaspora Literacy, not simply as an academic pursuit, but as a way of life—one that affirms the brilliance, resilience, and humanity of Black children across generations and geographies. By centering their stories, histories, and voices, we cultivate classrooms and communities where Black children are not merely included, but profoundly loved. In doing so, we join a collective legacy of educators, families, and freedom fighters who insist that loving Black children unapologetically is both the foundation and the future of our work.

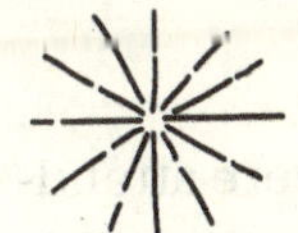

Introduction

Gloria Swindler Boutte, Joyce E. King,
George L. Johnson, Jr., LaGarrett J. King,
and Jarvais J. Jackson

We (Still) Be Lovin' Black Children[1]

Figure A. Adinkra symbol: *Odo nnyew fie kwan,* "love never loses its way home," a symbol of the power of love
Source: http://www.adinkra.org/htmls/adinkra/odon.htm

In the tradition of African culture, we welcome you. This book is *pro*-Black. Pro-Black does not mean *anti*-white or *anti* anything else. It means that this little book is about what we as Black people must do to ensure that Black children across the world are loved and safe and that their souls and spirits are healed from the ongoing damage of living in a world in which white supremacy flourishes. We hope you can endorse that. To be clear, Black children—wherever they are in the world and regardless if they are in majority Black settings or not—need to learn Black history. This book offers insights and tips about how we can make sure that they do. At the time the first edition was written, the world was experiencing the

1   During a brainstorming conference at the Conference on African Diaspora Literacy in 2019, Tambra Jackson suggested this title. There was unanimous agreement among the group.

COVID-19 health pandemic, and many children were attending school virtually or via a hybrid learning situation. This book helped support children and parents during this time.

This is a love book (see Figure A for the Adinkra symbol for love), and we want you to read and share it with as many Black people as you can so that collectively we can become literate about our shared culture. We also welcome others to join us in becoming literate in this way. We call this type of literacy, knowledge, and understanding *African Diaspora Literacy*. This information can literally serve to heal Black people from historical and contemporary trauma that we collectively experience. One thing we know for sure is that no cultural group can survive if they do not know and embrace their history. If you want to learn how to use Black love as a healing salve, then this is the book for you.

Before you put this book down because you think that the language in the title, *We Be Lovin' Black Children*, is not what you expected, let us explain why we chose to use African American Language. African American Language (also called Ebonics, Black English, and other names) is the most distinct dialect in the United States. Despite what you may have heard, it is a highly sophisticated language with distinct features that other dialects do not have. For example, it has five present verb tenses and unique features and uses of words like *be*. That *be* is so powerful that it can mean the past, the present, and the future. Linguists refer to it as the *habitual be*. So when we say that *we **be** lovin' Black children*, it means that we loved them in the *past*, we love them in the *present*, and we will love them in the *future*. No one can make us *not* love them. We love them 24/7—all day, seven days a week; 365/366 days a year. That is deep love, and that is why we wrote this book.

Around the world, there are parallel forms of African American Language—in the United States, Africa, the Caribbean, South America, and so forth. We are proud of this rich language heritage just as we are proud of Black children. The lives and welfare of our children and future generations are in danger if we, as adults, do not help them learn and value their history and understand contemporary issues that affect us all as Black people. The goal of this book is to share the wisdom that we have learned as professors and teachers—and parents. At the same time, we recognize the wisdom among Black people from all walks of life in families, communities, social and political organizations, and educational institutions. Collectively, we can use our love for Black children to make the world a better, safer, and more humane place for them.

How Deep Is Your Love?

The lack of knowledge is darker than the night.

—African Proverb

The preceding African proverb captures what happened to Black people when our ancestors were first brought to the United States and brutally enslaved. White enslavers intentionally and forcefully tried to remove our ancestors' knowledge of anything they knew about their cultures, histories, and identities while brutally exploiting the knowledge and skills that made their labor valuable. The proverb also conveys what has happened to Black people in other places who were colonized by Europeans. This book will help adults and children begin thinking about how to re-member (or put back together) the parts of our heritage that enslavers, laws, mores, and cultural domination intentionally and systematically sought to take from Black people—and still do.

The education of any people should begin with the people themselves, but Negroes thus trained have been dreaming about the ancients of Europe and about those who have tried to imitate them. (Woodson, 1933/1990, p. 32)

This book is intended to be a resource and reference to be consulted often. It contains a wealth of ideas that families, educators, and community members can use to teach Black children and heal them. Please share it widely. Don't be surprised or misled by people who discourage reading the book and engaging Black children in these activities. Remember that there are many people who (1) do not realize that Black children's spirits and psyches are being damaged daily in school and society and (2) do not have Black children's and people's best interest in mind—well-meaning intentions notwithstanding. We hope you will not be deterred by "haters" and that you will do your part to ensure that Black children everywhere know that they are *young, gifted, and Black—and have their souls intact*. This little book could well be the most important book you will ever read.

Finally, we acknowledge the Spencer Foundation's support for the conference on African Diaspora Literacy in September 2019. This book emerged from a 2-day working conference that convened 30 people, including educational researchers, P-12 classroom teachers, and a community member. Participants were multi-ethnic, multigenerational, international, and multidisciplinary (e.g., from disciplines such as history, social studies, economics, English, African studies, education foundations, early childhood education, secondary education). All attendees were connected via the Center for the Education and Equity of African American Students (www.ceeaas.com). Faculty participants were from historically Black colleges and universities, predominantly white institutions, and international institutions (representing six African diasporic countries—Cameroon, Ghana, Jamaica, Mali, Nigeria, and South Africa). The primary goal was to think together about how to ensure Black people's welfare in the United States and globally. The conference provided a platform for strategizing how best to amplify work on African Diaspora Literacy and increase its visibility. An important goal was to figure out how to make the scholarship on African Diaspora Literacy accessible to the wider population beyond educators. This book is an attempt to do so. After you read it, we hope that you will not only feel more informed, but you will also feel a more profound sense of joy about *lovin' Black children and youth*. Happy reading! Stay well.

References

Woodson, C. G. (1933/1990). The Mis-Education of the Negro. The Associate Publishers.

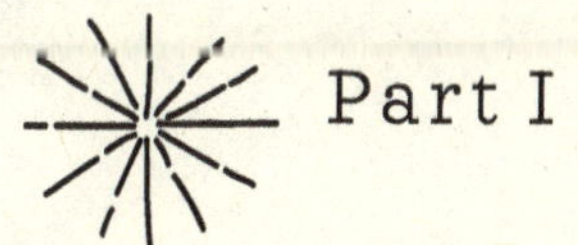 Part I

BLACK FOLKS IN THE UNITED STATES

Open Love Letter to Black Families and Communities

Dear Black Families and Community Members,

We still be lovin' Black children!

WE (Black people everywhere) still be lovin' Black children.

We **STILL** (continuously) be lovin' Black children.

We still **BE** (perpetually) lovin' Black children.

We still be **LOVIN'** (unapologetically, even through

our fears) Black children.

We still be lovin' **BLACK** children.

Drawing from African cosmologies, we speak these words three times to affirm the wholeness of life cycles—*Past, Present, Future*—and to honor the continuity of existence. In African worldviews, life is a circle: *Birth - Life - Death* - and beyond. The Malawian proverb reminds us, *"The only thing more precious than our children are our children's children."* This truth calls us to a profound commitment, not just to the children before us, but to the generations they will birth, nurture, and protect.

In the first edition of this book, we unpacked what *We be lovin' Black children* means—loving Black children perpetually in past, present, and future. In this second edition, we go further: What does this LOVE look like? How do we, as adults, show up for Black children in ways that strengthen their spirits? We begin this love letter with a pressing question:

Are you bequeathing your children—or the children you work with—a legacy of fear?

If the answer is yes, how does that legacy serve them? Even when we do not realize it, our children are watching, listening, and absorbing our fears. They know. They feel. Are our children carrying anxieties about what will happen to them simply because they are Black? And if so, what are we doing to buffer, uplift, and redirect that trajectory toward life-affirming possibilities?

We began with fear because we have seen how deeply it threads through our intergenerational lives. For instance, too often, Black adults are hesitant—even afraid—to say certain words out loud, such as *Pro-Black*. Here are other examples we have observed.

- Some people avoid saying "Black" or "African American" to describe themselves, instead choosing coded phrases like *"people who look like me."*

- Many whisper the word *"white"* (e.g., *"Was he white?"*)—as though naming whiteness itself is forbidden.

These silences are signs of trauma, reminders of the ways fear has been planted in us across generations. And yet, while we acknowledge that fear is real and that every human carries fear, this book insists that fear does not get the last word. Our collective charge is to act in intentional, Pro-Black ways that keep Black children's spirits intact—*despite* our fear. Our children will suffer if we allow fear to paralyze us.

And so, even as fear lingers, we must remember that fear is not our inheritance; LOVE is. Fear constricts, but love expands. Fear silences, but love gives voice. Fear diminishes, but love restores. To love Black children Pro-Blackly is to do more than whisper encouragement. It is to model courage. It means:

- **Naming Blackness boldly.** Saying *Black* out loud, without apology, shame, or hesitation.

- **Affirming Black children daily.** Speaking into existence their brilliance, their creativity, and their capacity to lead.

- **Protecting Black children's spirits.** Creating homes, classrooms, and communities where they feel safe to dream, to stumble, to question, and to grow.

- **Connecting Black children to their lineages.** Reminding them that they come from ancestors who dreamed them into being, survived the unimaginable, and left us blueprints for thriving.

- **Envisioning futures with Black children.** Not only preparing them to "make it" in this world, but to *change it*—to be architects of new worlds where freedom and justice are not slogans but lived realities.

This is what Pro-Black love looks like in action—walking beside Black children, not ahead of them or behind them, but *with* them—protecting, guiding, and cheering them on as they carry the torch forward. Our love letter, then, is also a call.

- **Let us not hand down fear as our legacy.**

- **Let us bequeath courage.**

- **Let us sow joy.**

- **Let us cultivate hope.**

- **Let us live in ways that make Black children believe, without question, that they are loved, cherished, and free to soar.**

In African cosmologies, time is never linear; it is a circle. The past lives within us, the present demands our attention, and the future calls us forward. Our children are not separate from this circle—they are the living bridge between ancestors and descendants yet unborn.

When we say *We be lovin' Black children*, we are not only speaking to the ones before us today. We are speaking to their ancestors who dreamed them here and to their children's children who will carry the song onward. To love Black children is to honor this sacred continuum.

So we return to where we began: **We still be lovin' Black children**. Fiercely. Perpetually. Unapologetically. In the face of fear, in the midst of joy, across generations. Past. Present. Future. May this be the legacy we leave—not a cycle of fear, but a circle of love so expansive that it enfolds every Black child, everywhere, always. Because we recognize that what you don't know *can* hurt you (and our children), the remainder of this chapter alerts you to anti-Black violence that exists in schools and offer a few Pro-Black remedies.

In Solidarity,
Kamania Wynter and Gloria Swindler Boutte
Black Mother Scholars

Anti-Black Violence in Schools

When someone tells you who they are, believe them the first time.

—Maya Angelou

And yet, even as we surround Black children with love, we cannot ignore the violence that assaults them daily in schools. To love them is to name and resist these violences—physical, symbolic, curricular, linguistic, and systemic—that threaten their very spirits. Bettina Love, teacher educator at Teachers College–Columbia University, explains that from the moment our Black children enter the school doors, their *spirits* are murdered on a daily basis. To be clear, the types of violence that we share (physical, symbolic, linguistic, curricular/instructional, and systemic) are often disguised and difficult to see. Indeed, they could be classified as being *passive-aggressive*. But just as white children are not overtly told that they are superior to others (even though the textbooks include disproportionate stories about their history, heroes, and heroines, and so forth), Black children are not always directly given the message that they are thought of as inferior. Yet the messages are clear and are ingested by our children without them knowing it.

Below, we share a few examples of the five types of violence in schools (physical, symbolic, linguistic, curricular/instructional, and systemic), which may escape your notice. Even if your child does not experience all five types of violence, they witness them, which has its own psychological damage.

- **Symbolic violence looks like** attacks on Black children's psyches, spirits, and humanity through negative stereotypes and silencing. For example, in 2017 Black mother April Carr's son was targeted by a teacher who pretended to shoot him with a gun-shaped object in class (Phillips, 2017). Symbolic violence also shows up daily when Black children's voices and experiences are ignored, erased, or dismissed. Ever hear Black children say they do not like their skin color?

- **Systemic violence shows up when** school structures, policies, and practices disproportionately harm Black children. African American students are over-referred to special education, suspended, and expelled at much higher rates than their non-Black peers—even in preschool (Washington Post, 2016). Systemic violence is embedded in tracking, zero-tolerance policies, overcrowded schools, and chronic underfunding. Ever hear Black children say other Black children are "bad" or "don't know how to behave in school"?

- **Physical violence looks like** outright attacks on Black children's bodies. In October 2015 a 16-year-old Black girl in South Carolina was violently thrown from her desk by a school resource officer while her classmates watched (Barajas, 2015). Ever hear Black children say they are afraid of the police?

- **Curricular and instructional violence shows up when** what and how children are taught normalizes whiteness and distorts or erases Black histories and contributions. Examples include a mock "slave auction" staged by a New York teacher and a Civil War reenactment in Georgia (Griffith, 2019). Black history is too often mistaught, sanitized, or omitted, leaving children with the message that Black people have contributed little of value. Ever hear Black children say that Black people are not smart?

- **Linguistic violence looks like** policing Black children's language and devaluing African American language or other home languages. It appears in corrections that shame children for how they speak, in classrooms where Black linguistic genius is ignored, and in curricula that frame Standardized English as the only legitimate form of communication. Ever hear Black children say, "I don't talk right"?

Can Black History Heal Our Children?

In our previous works, we have argued that learning African and African American history serves as an antidote to the ongoing violence Black children face in schools. It is not enough to only name the harm; we must also offer tools that actively nurture and heal our children.

Strengthen your Pro-Black journey by building networks with other families and community members. This work is deeply joyful, but also demanding, and it should never be carried alone. Surround yourself with people you trust, and together begin planning ways to confront anti-Blackness at both personal and institutional levels. To sustain the work and the people in it, rotate leadership within the group so that no single person is overburdened and everyone's gifts can shine.

We present a few *starter* ideas for healing our children. Many others are available via an internet search. Our hope is that families will become excited and locate a world of resources to teach Black history. We encourage families and community members to be creative and teach Black history in engaging and interactive ways. The lessons and activities do not have to be long or formal. For instance, you can teach while driving children to school and to extracurricular activities. Importantly, Black history needs to be ongoing, taught, and re-taught.

1. **Character Development Using Adinkra Symbols.** To counter symbolic and curricular violence, use Adinkra symbols from West Africa to teach African principles and values that have guided Black people since Ancient

Africa to contemporary times for Black people worldwide (http://www.adinkra.org/htmls/adinkra_index.htm). Have children identify Adinkra symbols and values that are important to them (e.g., courage, perseverance, loyalty, wisdom). Find character traits of African and African American people historically and presently. One source is the Smithsonian National Museum of African American History and Culture on social media (https://nmaahc.si.edu/explore/stories).

2. **Reading.** To counter curricular violence, intentionally and routinely provide books and other media that liberate the Black spirit by providing stories written by Black authors and including Black people's perspectives through every historical period.

3. **Africa.** We emphasize that Black history starts in Africa—not with enslavement. Our children need to know that Africa is the cradle of civilization and need to unlearn many negative myths about Africa. We suggest using works of fiction and nonfiction. During every historical and contemporary period, focus on African principles of wisdom, perseverance, self-determination, and Black people's other strengths (see Appendix A). Over time, try to teach information from the following six overlapping historical periods (Boutte et al., 2016). Your children will get the idea of how Black people's strengths have endured across time and space.

- Ancient Africa (e.g., Ethiopia, Kush, Kemet, Ghana, Mali, Songhay)—Remember the earliest humans are from Africa

- Enslavement (1500s–1865)—textbooks will say 1619 (research this)

- Reconstruction (1865–1877)

- Jim Crow/Segregation (1890–1965/1970)

- Civil Rights/Black Nationalism (1954–1968)

- Contemporary African American and African Life and Realities (1969–present)

Consider beginning with a geography lesson of the seven continents and then learn more in-depth information about Africa. For example, the song *In My Africa* teaches about the 54 (now 55) countries in Africa and how they are diverse (https://www.youtube.com/watch?v=pYh-zW3UkS8).

You can focus on ancient Kemet (Egypt) and the Ma'at principles: truth, justice, balance, order, compassion, harmony, and reciprocity through discussion, read alouds, and research. Likewise, it is always fascinating to know that Africa is the cradle of *all* civilization and to study ancient kingdoms so we understand many of the legacies present among African American people today. Children will enjoy role-playing and dressing up as kings, queens, and other citizens in Ancient Africa. They will be delighted to learn that the richest man to ever live (to date) was Mansa Musa from Mali.

Final Thoughts—Overcoming Fear . . . For Our Children

The thing to do is grab the broom of anger and drive off the beast of fear.

—Zora Neale Hurston

Presently, as we watch Black children being separated from their histories, we seek to re-energize and mobilize Black people to stand up and protect our children. We write with an intergenerational urgency that calls for Black people to collectively overcome our fears and protect Black children, our children, at all costs and by any means necessary.

Many Black people are repelled by scenes of African American people being whipped, lynched, or otherwise abused during slavery. Yet we barely blink in the midst of endemic and ongoing spirit murders (Love, 2016) of our children in schools that are taking place in plain view. Indeed, few of us recognize it. Even the best of us fall short amid ongoing violence against our children—especially in schools where they are suspended, expelled, placed in special education, demeaned, made invisible in the curriculum.

In the Black community, we LOVE our children. As we eagerly await them, we give them strong and meaningful, loving names like Stephanie, Jonathan, Janiyah, Jaliyah, Carter, Layla, Dylan, and Langston. We try to protect them—sending them to church, encouraging them to do well in school, carefully selecting their friends, sometimes moving to new neighborhoods if we can afford it. Yet most of us often forget to give them what they need the most to thrive, heal, and survive in a world driven by white supremacy. We fail to teach them their history. In this book, we explain how this can be a fatal oversight in terms of premature death of our children to violence and lifelong, generational damage. This book is based on foundational African legacies that have sustained Black people worldwide since the beginning of time to now (Appendix A). Learn also about principles for Black education (Appendix B).

Please do not put this book down if you care about Black children. This is a *pro*-Black book. This is an urgent call to Black families and communities. Recognizing that we are all interconnected, we ask what are we willing to do not only for our own biological, adopted, or related children, but for all Black children? Letting our ancestors have the final word, we close this chapter with a collective chorus from Ancestors Hurston, Lorde, and King.

Your silence will not protect you.

—Audre Lorde

There comes a time when silence is betrayal.

—Rev. Dr. Martin Luther King, Jr.

If you are silent about your pain, they'll kill you and say you enjoyed it.

—Zora Neale Hurston

In the end, we will remember not the words of our enemies, but the silence of our friends.

—Rev. Dr. Martin Luther King, Jr.

References

Barajas, J. (2015, October 27). S.C. school resource officer fired after he drags student, sheriff says. *PBS News*. https://www.pbs.org/newshour/nation/south-carolina-video

Boutte, G. S., Johnson, G. L., Wynter-Hoyt, K., & Uyoata, U. E. (2017). Using African Diaspora Literacy to heal and restore the souls of Black folks. *International Critical Childhood Policy Studies Journal, 6*(1), 66–79.

Griffith, J. (2019, May 29). Black students were cast as slaves in New York teacher's mock 'auctions,' state finds. *NBC News*. https://www.nbcnews.com/news/nbcblk/black-students-were-cast-slaves-new-york-teacher-s-mock-n1011361

Love, B. L. (2016). Anti-Black state violence, classroom edition: The spirit murdering of Black children. *Journal of Curriculum and Pedagogy, 13*(1), 22–25.

Phillips, K. (2017, November 7). 'That's how people like you get shot': Video shows high school teacher threatening his student. *Washington Post*. https://www.washingtonpost.com/news/education/wp/2017/11/07/thats-how-people-like-you-get-shot-video-shows-high-school-teacher-threatening-his-student/

Washington Post. (2016, October 8). Racial profiling in preschool. https://www.washingtonpost.com/news/education/wp/2017/11/07/thats-how-people-like-you-get-shot-video-shows-high-school-teacher-threatening-his-student/

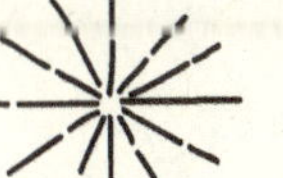

2

Gloria Swindler Boutte, Jarvais J. Jackson,
George L. Johnson, Janice Baines,
and Nicole Y. Strange-Martin

Pro-Blackness: What It Looks Like and What It Is

We stand in awe of the courage of Anna Julia Cooper (1892), Dr. W. E. B. Du Bois (1903), and Dr. Carter G. Woodson(1933), whose unapologetically Pro-Black writings—*A Voice from the South, The Souls of Black Folk*, and *The Miseducation of the Negro*—emerged during the height of the Jim Crow era. Their words challenged a society intent on silencing Black thought and erasing Black humanity. Today, more than a century later, we are called to summon that same boldness on behalf of Black children—and on behalf of ourselves.

Pro-Blackness: What It Looks Like

You may be wondering: *What does Pro-Blackness mean?* In Black culture, we don't always hand you neat, dictionary-style answers (Boutte, 2015). Our language is layered. Sophisticated. Metaphorical. We make you think. We make you *feel.*

> Take Patricia McKissack's (1986) *Flossie and the Fox*:
> Flossie asked Big Mama, "How do a fox look?"
> Now—Big Mama could have said,

Fur. Pointed ears. Sharp nose.
But she didn't.

She said,
"Chile, a fox be just a fox.
But one thing for sure—
that rascal loves eggs.
He'll do most anything to get some eggs."

And just like that,
Flossie knew.
If she saw something eyeing her basket,
it wasn't just any animal—
it was a fox.

That's how Black wisdom works. Full of verve, energy, imagination. More powerful than plain words on a page. And that's how we talk about Pro-Blackness—not as a dry definition, but through the lives of those who showed us. In the same spirit of understanding through inference and a real example, we illustrate Pro-Blackness through the courageous work of Cooper, Du Bois, and Woodson.

- **Anna Julia Cooper**—In the 1880s, as a teacher, she insisted on the highest levels of achievement for her Black students. This was far from the norm, yet she persisted with uncompromising conviction.

- **W. E. B. Du Bois**—Together with Jessie Fauset and Augustus Dill, he launched *The Brownies' Book* in 1920, the first magazine in the United States created specifically for African American children. Though short-lived (1920–1921), it was groundbreaking in affirming Black children's worth, creativity, and cultural pride.

- **Carter G. Woodson**—As early as 1922, he began publishing and distributing textbooks, pamphlets, and booklets on Black history for schools and churches. What makes this astonishing is the context: During the Jim Crow era, in a hostile environment without internet, legal protections, or institutional support, Woodson's materials were widely circulated, taught, and embraced—often fugitively and defiantly (Givens, 2021).

This is Pro-Blackness.
Not a theory. Not a slogan.
It is a way of moving.
A way of creating.
A way of protecting Black life—
even when the world tries to shut it down.

Pro-Blackness—What It Is

Okay, for those of you who still need a formalized definition, here it is. First, we note that *anti-Blackness* was described in Chapter 1. We intentionally choose not to live in the headspace of *anti-Blackness* and don't want to conjure that spirit. We need to be aware of anti-Blackness for sure, but we want to live in the space of *Pro-Blackness*. Every time we say a word, we give it energy and life. You are likely thinking, *When are they going to define Pro-Blackness?* Rushing us is so non-Pro-Black by the way. Sorry, we just bein' Black.

Pro-Blackness is an unapologetic, positive, proactive perspective regarding Blackness and Black people (Boutte et al., 2024). When we say Black people we mean all Black people; with all of the intersections that come along. *Pro* connotes advocating for Blackness. It does not mean *anti*-white—or any other ethnic group. Damn, we can't have anything! Pro-Blackness should not be misinterpreted to mean that we focus solely on Black children (Boutte & Compton-Lilly, 2022). To make it plain, if we say we love purple, that does not mean that we dislike other colors or only love the color purple. In order to protect Black children, we *must* dedicate time to loving them in ways that are intentional and focused. This goes beyond naïve and emotional ways of loving children to revolutionary love, designed to protect their humanity (Boutte et al., 2023).

We understand that Black people identify and show up in many different ways, often carrying identities that are layered, complex, and at times even contradictory (Boutte, 2022). Blackness is not one-dimensional; it is multispirited, textured, and alive. Some may carry their Blackness quietly, almost apologetically. Others embrace an African-centered worldview, standing firmly in cultural traditions and practices. Still others move through the world with a double-consciousness, navigating both the gaze of others and their own sense of self. And there are those whose Blackness feels hidden, muted, or almost erased through assimilation—an erasure that comes at a great personal cost. What remains clear is that to deny or suppress Blackness is to deny a vital part of one's being, and such denial works against the wholeness, wellness, and liberation that Black people deserve.

Pro-Blackness conveys Black in a positive manner. Basically, you should recognize it when you see and feel it. We share **four** examples of high quality Pro-Black programs that can guide others who *love Black children*: (1) *Drs. Diaspora* Saturday School Curriculum and Tours to Africa; (2) Black Education Research Center (BERC); (3) The Children's Defense Fund Freedom Schools; and (4) the Black Girls Code. After reading this book, we expect an abundance of Pro-Black programs (from readers) for Black children.

Drs. Diaspora Saturday School Curriculum and Tours to Africa

Drs. Diaspora is an afterschool/Saturday school curriculum that focuses on the historical and contemporary culture, history, and language of people in the African Diaspora. Developed by Drs. Gloria Boutte and George Johnson (aka Drs. Diaspora), the curriculum focuses on cultural continuity and uses African Diaspora Literacies (e.g., orality, music, dance, communalism) and can be adaptive for use in K-12 classes. The *Drs. Diaspora* curriculum addresses interdisciplinary content (e.g., history, art, literacy, mathematics, science) across six historical periods.

1. Ancient Africa and the African continent

2. Enslavement—Particular attention is paid to slave narratives, agency, and resistance of African people who were enslaved

3. Reconstruction

4. Jim Crow—including the Harlem Renaissance in the 1920s

5. Civil Rights Era—Emphasis on Black nationalism, freedom schools, freedom songs, and student protests

6. Contemporary Life in the United States and Africa Diaspora globally

Drs. Diaspora also does tours to Africa for youth and adults. For additional information, contact drsdiaspora@gmail.com or visit the LovinBlackChildren.com website.

Black Education Research Center

Housed at Teachers College, Columbia University, the Black Education Research Center advances Black, African-centered thought into research, policy, and practice. BERC created a first of its kind, district-wide PK-12 Black Studies curriculum for the New York City Public Schools. The *Black*

Studies As The Study Of The World: A PK-12 Black Studies Curriculum for New York City Public Schools is designed to be a standards-based pathway for integrating Black Studies into PK-12 classrooms. It offers interdisciplinary, culturally affirming lessons on African civilizations, the African Diaspora, Black life in America and New York, and local histories.

The included lessons are paced with NYC public schools' social studies scope and sequence anchored using the SCALE framework (Self-Knowledge; Culture; Agency; Leadership; Ethics/Values). The SCALE Framework for Learning and Liberation guides learners to reflect deeply on five guiding questions: (1) Who am I? (2) What do I believe? (3) What can I do? (4) How do I lead others? and (5) What do I value? These lessons are uniquely designed to invoke critical self-reflection and reconciliation. The *Black Studies as the Study of the World* is available at: https://www.tc.columbia.edu/berc/curriculum/. Other programs will find BERC's curriculum to be a useful guide.

Freedom Schools

The Children's Defense Fund (CDF) Freedom Schools started in 1964 as a summer program that organized Black college students for voting rights. Now, it serves as a summer program that builds literacy, self-esteem, socio-emotional skills, and a love of learning rooted in culturally affirming books and curricula. College students serve as teachers, mentors, and role models, all of whom are trained to implement a reading curriculum centered around a curated book list. CDF Freedom Schools are located across the United States seeking to advance the well-being of children and families.

Four of Drs. Boutte and Johnson's grandchildren attended Summer Freedom schools for several years—even during the COVID pandemic. Each day, they eagerly attended, were actively engaged, and could not wait for the next day. They could be heard singing Freedom School chants like "Good Job" or singing "Something Inside (So Strong)" daily. If schools were designed using Freedom School models, Black children will strive. In the meantime, community members interested in starting freedom school summer programs should reach out to the Children's Defense Fund Freedom Schools. https://www.childrensdefense.org/our-work/cdf-freedom-schools/.

Black Girls Code

Black Girls Code originated in 2011 to introduce Black girls and young women to technology professionals in Science, Technology, Engineering, and Mathematics (STEM), while concentrating on increasing the number of Black women represented in the STEM field. The nonprofit organization offers an array of free and paid programs such as boot camps, summer camps, webinars, and workshops for Black girls. Participants who attend these authentically developed opportunities are exposed to programming centers focused on teaching skills in web design, mobile app development, robotics, and more. Today, *Black Girls Code* has grown into an international nonprofit that aims to position and engage one million girls of color by 2040 in computer programming and careers in tech.

Black Girls Code has locations in multiple cities throughout the United States. This nonprofit organization has empowered young Black women from ages 7 to 19. Some participants are recruited and begin early. In the initial stages, *Black Girls Code* intrigues the growing minds of elementary girls. *Black Girls Code* develops the leadership proficiencies and talents in middle and high school girls in order to construct a distinct journey. Moreover, coding education transforms the next generation of leaders in tech professionals.

Conclusion

Pro-Blackness is more than words—it is action, imagination, and love that protects and uplifts Black life. From Cooper, Du Bois, and Woodson to today's community-based programs, Pro-Blackness shows us what is possible when we commit to nurturing Black brilliance. The charge is clear: Embody Pro-Blackness boldly, consistently, and unapologetically.

References

Boutte, G. S. (2015). Kindergarten through grade 3: Four things to remember about African American language: Examples From children's books. *Young Children, 70*(4), 38–45.

Boutte, G. S. (2022). *Educating African American students: And how are the children?* Routledge.

Boutte, G. S., & Compton-Lilly, C. (2022). Prioritizing Pro-Blackness in literacy research, scholarship, and teaching. *Journal of Early Childhood Literacy, 22*(3), 323–334.

Boutte, G. S., Jackson, J. J., Collins, S. N., Baines, J. R., Broughton, A., & Johnson, G. L. (2024). *Pro-Blackness in early childhood education: Diversifying curriculum and pedagogy in K-3 classrooms.* Teachers College Press.

Boutte, G., Wynter-Hoyte, K., & Bryan, N. (2023). *Revolutionary love for early childhood classrooms: Nurturing the brilliance of young Black children.* Scholastic Incorporated.

Cooper, A. J. (1892). *A voice from the South by a Black woman of the South.* Aldine Printing House.

Du Bois, W. E. B. (1903). *The souls of Black folk.* A. C. McClurg & Co.

Givens, J. R. (2021). *Fugitive pedagogy: Carter G. Woodson and the art of Black teaching.* Harvard University Press.

McKissack, P. (1986). *Flossie and the fox.* Penguin.

Woodson, C. G. (1933). *The mis-education of the Negro.* Associated Publishers.

*LaGarrett J. King, Dawnavyn James, Abigail Henry,
Gregory Simmons, and Daphanie Bibbs*

We Be Lovin' Black History: Eight Best Teaching Practices Around Black History Education

It goes without saying, but Black history education is important for the livelihood of Black children. Black history education for Black children enhances academic engagement, strengthens racial and cultural identity, boosts critical thinking and criticality, increases racial diaspora literacy development, and provides joy to name a few. However, the typical Black history education in K-12 schools is problematic. Black history curriculum attends to a handful of Black historical figures such as Martin Luther King Jr., Rosa Parks, and Harriet Tubman and historical events such as slavery, Reconstruction, and the Civil Rights Movement. Many times, these narratives are superficial, not comprehensive, and whitewashed, typically not detailing the complete truth as to what has happened or who these people are. Some argue that Black history in K-12 schools is developed to be non-threatening to white society. This is what Carter G. Woodson (1933) has called, and we have repurposed, as "miseducation."

Many teachers are products of miseducation and cannot or will not expand past the absent and superficial narratives.

Anti-Black history education policies, standards, and politics also contribute to the lack of Black history teaching. This has led to many Black parents, community educators, and other Black history advocates taking the lead to teach Black history to Black children.

To aid in teaching Black history, we, The Center for K-12 Black History and Racial Literacy Education, have developed a few best practices for teaching Black history to Black children, guided by Black historical consciousness (BHC). Black Historical Consciousness, developed by LaGarrett King (2020), is a set of curricular and instructional principles that guide Black history education. Teaching with BHC in mind is to teach *through* Black history and not *about* Black history. That means Black history should be taught through the experiences, perspectives, and voices of Black people. Below we share the eight principles of Black Historical Consciousness (see Figure 3.1) and provide some suggestions as to how we can approach Black history topics with these principles in mind. These eight principles can be instructive to anyone who teaches Black history. They are not intended to be presented linearly or one by one but should be integrated throughout the teachings.

Best Teaching Practices Around Black History Education Using Black Historical Consciousness

1. **Power, Oppression, and Anti-Blackness** addresses the lack of justice, freedom, equality, and equity experienced by Black people throughout history. Due to the omnipresent occurrence of anti-Blackness throughout society, this principle requires that teachers connect historical content and sources to the history of racism, power, and privilege. Teachers must be prepared to address students' racialized experiences when exposed to this principle, by not avoiding discussions that are challenging. Racial literacy is required to

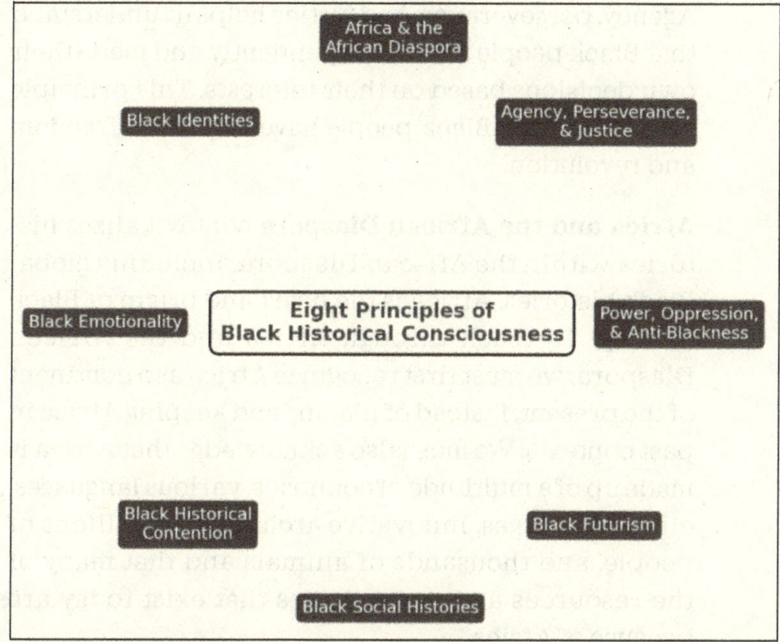

Figure 3.1. Eight Principles of Black Historical Consciousness

describe issues of power, oppression, and white suppression and its lasting legacy today. Lastly, this principle must be combined with Pro-Blackness through the use of any other principle, most notably, agency, perseverance, and justice.

2. **Agency, Perseverance, and Justice** acknowledges that although victimized, Black people were (and are) not helpless. They fought/fight against oppression for their freedom throughout all historical eras, both proactively and reactively. It is important to set the foundation that Black people were their own people, divorced of who did something to them. The principle emphasizes that throughout history, Black people held power over who they are and what they would be.

Agency, perseverance, and justice helps us understand that Black people acted independently and made their own decisions based on their interests. This principle recognizes that Black people have a spirit of freedom and revolution.

3. **Africa and the African Diaspora** contextualizes histories within the African Diaspora, including global Black histories. Africa is the heart and origin of Black history. To teach through Africa and the African Diaspora, we must first recognize Africa as a continent of the present, instead of placing and keeping Africa in past contexts. We must also acknowledge that Africa is made up of a multitude of countries, various languages, climate changes, innovative architecture, billions of people, and thousands of animals and that many of the resources and technologies that exist today are because of Africa.

    The key words of this principle are *Africa* and *diaspora*. To teach these concepts, educators must first (re)define diaspora and differentiate what they know and assume about Africa and what they must unlearn about Africa. Giving students the opportunity to chart their knowledge, assumptions, and misconceptions of Africa gives educators an assessment into what needs to be taught. Showing a variety of diasporic maps that illustrate the spread and separation of Africans from Africa allows students to see how Black people exist across the world in other continents like South America, Europe, and North America.

    The most important task for educators and students learning through this principle is to understand that Black people, history, and culture exist outside of the United States. Reading books written by Haitian and Jamaican authors, teaching about Black History

Month celebrations in different countries, honoring Afro-Latinx historical figures, or analyzing the works of African artists gives students a diasporic view of Blackness and expands their knowledge of Black history to give them a more global perspective. Importantly, we must teach that African Diasporic people everywhere are culturally interconnected.

4. **Black Identities** promotes the inclusion of Black identities beyond Black, middle-class, heterosexual, able-bodied, Christian men. A key to teaching through this principle is highlighting the unseen. By this we mean lesser-known Black perspectives such as those of women, queer, disabled, and more. By expanding the narratives beyond those that are acceptable to white people, this principle celebrates the diversity of Black peoples' experiences and encourages empathy to individuals whose biographies and beliefs may differ from our own. It is worth noting that resources, specifically primary sources, are often unavailable or not easily accessible for a teacher to teach through this principle. When this occurs, we encourage teachers to identify and ask students what other Black perspectives would help facilitate a more rigorous discussion of the Black history content being taught. By identifying people who were often unseen, educators help students recognize and honor all Black individuals.

One strategy for achieving this is to integrate the lives and work of Black women, queer and transgender activists, disabled leaders, working-class organizers, and a broader range of faith traditions. For instance, lessons can highlight the activism of Ella Baker in conjunction with Bayard Rustin or connect Fannie Lou Hamer's grassroots organizing with contemporary disability justice frameworks that continue to influence Black liberation. Incorporating the work of contemporary figures such as Audre Lorde, Barbara Smith, and the founders of recent social justice movements helps students understand how layered identities shape ongoing struggles for justice.

Ultimately, teaching Black history through an intersectional lens is about expanding representation and fostering critical consciousness. This pedagogical framework ensures that students move beyond a singular narrative of Blackness to instead recognize the richness, resilience, and multiplicity of Black life. It empowers learners to value all voices within the Black experience and to understand history as a dynamic, inclusive narrative.

5. **Black Emotionality** focuses on Black people's emotions, including joy, fear, rage, sadness, and hope. The key is to normalize Black people's humanity, the emotions that come from generations of oppression, and how we defied those oppressive structures of the time. Examples include family dynamics, Black music, dance, cultural expressions, sports, holidays and traditions, social unrest, and Black Arts Movements.

6. **Black Historical Contention** has two meanings. The first meaning is to understand that Black people were/are not a monolithic group throughout history and the present. We make mistakes when we assume that Black people have similar belief systems, cultures, and customs. Even when we teach Black histories centering on social justice, various Black communities approach civil rights and humanity differently. Many of these ideas were contentious to each other. For the most part, I believe teachers understand the phenomenon of Black

history teaching as littered with comparisons and contrasting elements between Booker T. Washington and W. E. B. Du Bois; Martin Luther King Jr. and Malcolm X; and the many other African American civil rights groups and their approaches towards liberation.

The second meaning is called the "do no wrong" history phenomenon where teaching Black history is more of a statement of moral superiority and respectability than an exploration of history. While educators may not say it directly, it is implied, through absent narratives, that Black people did not participate in trauma or harm throughout history. Black people throughout history have been guilty of many types of discrimination and phobias that have plagued global societies such as sexism, sexual harassment, homophobia, ethnic subjugation, and classism. So, when presenting Black history, both virtues and vices can be discussed, though caution should be noted with an overabundance of negative narratives since many exist widely in society.

7. **Black Social Histories** includes narratives of "regular" people (especially children) who have made (and are making) a difference in their communities. To teach through this principle is to teach and lift up those other than Black icons. By identifying the agency and commitments to improving Black communities of regular "Black" folk who help "to lift, as we climb," students can learn about the power of both individual and collective action. This principle invites teachers to identify local grassroots efforts from schools, religious organizations, nonprofits, and more, that sought to improve Black life by whatever means. By identifying such local and social histories, students can learn

how to be advocates for their own Black communities. This principle celebrates the stories and efforts of neighbors, co-workers, friends, and allies.

8. **Black Futurism** is the concept that uses Black history knowledge to identify long-standing problems or successes and uses knowledge of the past to solve contemporary and future problems. Futurism is about planning for future action. It is a principle that allows students to critically think about how issues or successes of the past influence current society. Students assess certain topics such as racial inequities, race-based gerrymandering, food deserts, and segregation and devise plans about how to solve these issues. The purpose here is to start students thinking like community, national, and international leaders early so they can do something about these inequities. While we believe this approach will strengthen them as adult leaders in the future, we also believe that this type of education will strengthen them as current student leaders.

Conclusion

Black historical consciousness is new and developing, so it is continually evolving. We caution that Black historical consciousness is not merely a framework, although it can be used as one. Black historical consciousness is a mindset about teaching Black history, not only as content but to see, understand, and celebrate Black humanity.

References

King, L. (2020). Black history is not American history: Toward a framework of Black historical consciousness. *Social Education, 84*(6), 335–341.

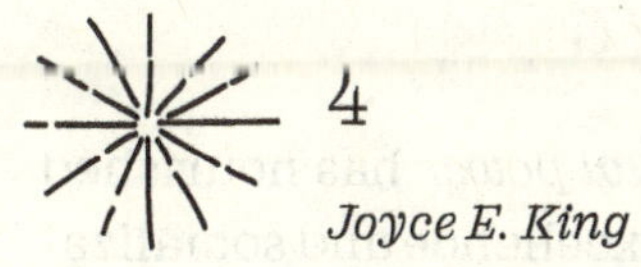

4

Joyce E. King

My Soul Looks Back in Wonder: What Are We Doing to "Serve the Present Age"?

Surely, humans have been chosen to bring good into the world.

—Odù Ifá, 78:1 Irosù Wòrì (Karenga, 1999, p. 228)

We sent thee as a mercy to all peoples.

—Holy Qur'an, S21:107

A charge to keep I have, a God to glorify

A never dying soul to save, and fit it for the sky

To serve the present age, my calling to fulfill …

—Charles Wesley (1707–1788)/African American Spiritual

Introduction

Being literate about the African Diaspora means understanding not only the history that is too often missing in curriculum and pedagogy but also the power of African peoples' profoundly spiritual heritage of critical-cultural-historical consciousness—especially in the way we respond in times of difficulty, trouble, and duress (Paris,

1984). Our heritage of African *spiritual power* has nourished the humanizing legacy of education excellence and socialization that African people here and there in the world inherit from our ancestors. Remembering the ethical teachings of our sages, we recognize our divine ancestral calling to "bring good into the world" (Fáláadé, 1998). We know that we *are* our ancestors—not just their "wildest dreams," but they live on and have their expression in us (Asante & Mazama, 2022, p. xxii). In this fraught present age, fearlessly and without equivocation: We (still) be lovin' Black children. Baba Asa G. Hilliard (2011) reminded us of our African power in the charge he gave us to fulfill: "To be African or Not to Be."

Weapons of the Soul

The contributors of this second edition share insights regarding our tradition of African power in education, which I suggest reflects our divinely inspired humanizing ancestral charge: Education *and* socialization in service to humanity. This power is preserved and is available to us in Black/African Diaspora thought and practice, in sacred and secular texts, in the intellectual truth-telling of Black Studies scholarship, in Black arts, dance, and music—from African American spirituals, for example: "If I could help somebody as I pass along the way . . ." (Gospel hymn)—to the blues: "When things go wrong, wrong with you, it hurts me, too" (Elmore James). These are our "weapons of the soul," cultural resources of resistance to domination that inform the pedagogical praxis presented in this volume (Larsen, 1996).

And my soul looks back in wonder as public education is being dismantled state by state, Black history in museums and National Park Service Black heritage sites are being whitewashed by presidential mandates, and censorship is the most visible element of what amounts to undeclared cultural warfare against Black education.

This chapter presents selected exemplars of Black/African Diaspora thought and practice to illustrate what some educators, including caregivers in school and community settings, elders, and family members, are doing, not within a Eurocentric values framework but from within the African-centered paradigm to prepare our children to serve humanity in this present age of the most pernicious threats to our survival since the nadir of Reconstruction. With our ancestor, the renowned Zulu High Sanusi (Priest) Vusamazulu Credo Mutwa, we, too, believe the remedy is education (Larsen, 1996, p. xxvi). Indeed, Watson-Vandiver and Wiggan (2021), in *The Healing Power of Education: Afrocentric Pedagogy* as a Tool for Restoration and Liberation, illuminate the role of ancestors in their discussion of education as self-healing power (p. xi). Dei, Karanja, and Erger (2022), affirming the important role of elders' knowledges, explore the question of Black/African Indigeneity in education. Embedded in the examples that follow is the wisdom of divine instruction as far back as ancient Kemet: "Know Yourself."

What We Are Doing to Serve the Present Age Here and There in the African Diaspora

Faith in Florida, a statewide nonprofit coalition of faith leaders, has created a downloadable Black history toolkit for religious leaders to provide comprehensive, alternative instruction on African American history in hundreds of congregational settings like churches, synagogues, and mosques, particularly in response to Florida's new state curriculum standards that require teachers to teach about the benefits of enslavement and tone down slavery's horrors. This initiative aims to counter censorship and ensure that truthful, accurate teaching about African American enslavement, systemic racism, and the Black freedom struggle are taught. Black ministers declare they will use the toolkit in Sunday School.[1]

---

1   Faith in Florida, https://www.faithinflorida.org/

George J. Sefa Dei, African-centered Education in Canada. Professor Dei, a founding scholar of Afrocentric education in Canada, is also a traditional chief among his people in Ghana. An activist African and Ghanaian Indigenous scholar who emigrated to Canada, he was also a leader in the establishment of the Toronto Board of Education's Africentric Alternative School in 2009. The community called for this school to address the high dropout rate and academic achievement gap among African ancestry students. Dei acknowledges that Afrocentricity "builds on the work and struggles of the radicals, the activists, the poets, the scholars, and the regular people in Africa and the Diaspora who have fought in their own ways against oppression" (Kempf & Dei, 2013, p. 790). [2]

Brazil's Black Movements

Public Law 10.639. Education has been central to the work of Brazil's Black Movements (Gonçalves e Silva, 2005). The 2003 Federal law 10.639 requires all public and private schools in Brazil to teach African and Afro-Brazilian history and culture. Implementation of the law has been erratic as teacher training and teaching materials are needed (Domingues, 2025).

African-Centered Psychology. Also, historically and politically significant are recent developments in African-centered Psychology in Brazil: A former student who studied with me and collaborated with other Black scholars here in the United States formed a study group in Brazil and translated *African Power*, Asa Hilliard's (2011) seminal text, into Portuguese (Nogueira et al., 2024).

Afrocentricity in Education. The first International Congress of Afrocentric Education convened in Bahia in May

---

2   Toronto District School Board Africentric Alternative School, https://www.tdsb.on.ca/Find-your/Details/schno/3949?display Module=Details%20of%20a%20School

2025, hosted by the State University of Bahia (UNEB) in partnership with The University of International Integration of the Afro-Brazilian Lusophony (UNILAB). The Congress was held in Salvador at several campus locations, and RoundTable sessions were also broadcast live on YouTube. The aim of the Congress was to promote connections between basic and higher education professionals, researchers, students, and activists from Brazil and other countries, and terreiro/Afro-Brazilian religious and quilombo leaders to share their knowledge and experiences regarding different dimensions of Afrocentric education practice in diverse educational settings. The program included mini-courses and paper presentations with simultaneous English–Portuguese translation. Attendees included professors from the United States and South Africa, as well as researchers, teachers, and students from various regions in Brazil. Professors Molefi Kete Asante (2023) and Nah Dove (2021) were among the invited speakers. The Congress is an initiative of the Aforcentrar Saúde Research Group: Ilera Dudu (UNEB) and the Afrocentric Education Research Group (Grupeafro/Unilab Malês), in partnership with the Education Laboratory for Ethnic-Racial Relations (UFPE) and the Afroperspectives, Knowledge, and Childhood Research Group (UFRRJ).[3]

Multimedia Activist Scholarship, Teaching, and Learning

Adbul Alkalimat (2021, 2022) has curated a comprehensive, interdisciplinary website and offered an online Black Studies

---

3   The announcement of the first International Congress of Afrocentric Education in English can be seen here: https://agenciadecomunicacao.uneb.br/uneb-e-unilab-realizam-primeiro-congresso-internacional-de-educacao-afrocentrada-de-05-a-09-de-maio/#:~:text=UNEB%20e%20Unilab%20realizam%20primeiro,de%20maio%20%2D%20Ag%C3%AAncia%20de%20Comunica%C3%A7%C3%A3o

course that "reflects three decades of work collecting, digitizing and sharing information and analysis that scholars, students, and the general public can use for free."[4]

In Class with Dr. Greg Carr (2011), promoted as "the largest Africana Studies Classroom in the world," is livestreamed Saturday mornings on YouTube, where Howard University Professor Greg Carr engages Pulitzer Prize–winning journalist/radio talk show host/educator Karen Hunter in conversation across a range of timely and historically significant topics.

Knarrative is Hunter's subscription-based global online community that provides members access to weekly "Office Hours" with Professor Greg Carr; an archive of 350+ online classes and interviews, available also as a podcast and other digital formats; and online Knarrative classes with seven other instructors.[5]

Black Studies Curricula in Public Schools and Teacher Preparation
New York City's Black Studies Curriculum. "Black Studies as the Study of the World" is a PK-12 Black Studies Curriculum developed at the Black Education Research Center (BERC) at Teachers College, Columbia University, led by Professor Sonya Douglass (Mokam, 2025). In addition to virtual professional learning programs for teachers, the 100 comprehensive lesson plans in the Black Studies Curriculum are aligned with New York State's Social Studies Standards and the Next Gen Standards for English Language Arts and History/Social Studies.[6]

---

4   Abdul Alkalimat, Scholar and Activist's Archive, https://www.alkalimat.org/websites.html

5   Knarrative, https://www.knarrative.com/

6   Black Education Research Center (BERC), Teachers College, Columbia University, https://www.tc.columbia.edu/berc/curriculum/

The California Black Studies Curriculum (CABSC). CABSC is based on the research of the state of California's (first in the nation) Reparations Task Force. University of California Berkeley Professors Travis J. Bristol and Tolani Britton in the Center for Research on Expanding Educational Opportunity (CREEO) led its development and community educators, parents, and high school students participated in the production of this California-centric 9th to 12th grade Black Studies curriculum. [7]

My California Reparations Task Force Expert Testimony. In April 2023, I submitted invited written testimony to the California Reparations Task Force (AB 3121) titled "Why We Need Black Studies Theory, Curriculum and Pedagogy in Teacher Preparation: The Evidence from K-12 to College to Professional Education Institutions." [8] After exhaustive investigation, the California Task Force final report endorsed the development of the California Black Studies Curriculum described above, which aligns with my testimony, recommendations, and a growing body of research (Acosta et al., 2017; Givens & Riddick, 2024; King, 2015, 2017). In my Task Force testimony I cited research showing that one of slavery's most traumatic legacies that denies Black students the safety and belonging they need to thrive in school is the way the "hard history" of slavery is taught—usually badly (King, 2019; Shuster et al., 2018).

Conclusion

Shujaa (1994) noted the particular importance of pedagogy, and Roane (2017) emphasizes its pedagogical mission as "one of the original aims of Black Studies":

---

7   California Black Studies Curriculum (CABSC), Center for Research on Expanding Educational Opportunity (CREEO), UC Berkeley, https://www.youtube.com/watch?v=XR9Nbre5oH8

8   California Reparations Report. See Chapter 6, "Separate and Unequal Education," https://oag.ca.gov/ab3121/report

> to inspire people to learn deeply and critically about the African Diasporas' histories and contemporary social formations; to develop an incisive critique of Western civilization; and to create and sustain black culture as an alternative source of power in a world fundamentally shaped by anti-black racism. (Roane, 2017)

We need only remember our heritage of African spiritual power that we have inherited to fortify ourselves with "weapons of the soul"—a praxis of critical-cultural-historical consciousness—to know ourselves and to protect Black children from the war we are facing, the fascism of this present age to be more precise.

CODA

Defeating fascism requires recognizing that we need to stand in solidarity and fight for others as if our lives depended on it.

—Robin D. G. Kelley, 2025, p. 23

The battlefront is everywhere. There is no sheltered rear.

—Paul Robeson, 1937

References

Acosta, M. M., Hudson-Vassel, C., Johnson, B., Cherfrere, G., Harris, M.G., Wallace, J., & Duggins, S. (2017). Beyond awareness: Black Studies for consciousness and praxis in teacher education. *Equity & Excellence in Education, 50*(2), 241–253.

Alkalimat, A. (2021). *The history of Black Studies*. Pluto Press.

Alkalimat, A. (2022). *The future of Black Studies*. Pluto Press.

Asante, M. K. (2023). *Revolutionary pedagogy: A primer for teachers of Black children* (2nd ed.). Universal Write Publications, LLC.

Asante, M. K., & Mazama, A. (2022). *Encyclopedia of African religion*. Sage.

Carr, G. (2011). What Black Studies is not: Moving from crisis to liberation in Africana intellectual work. *Socialism and Democracy, 25*(1), 178–191.

Dei, G. S., Karanja, W., & Erger, G. (2022). *Elders' cultural knowledges and the question of Black/African Indigeneity in education*. Springer.

Domingues, P. (2025). *Law 10.639/03 and the teaching of Afro-Brazilian history and culture*. Global Voices. https://globalvoices.org/2023/05/23/teaching-afro-brazilian-history-still-faces-challenges-despite-20-years-as-law/

Dove, N. (2021). *The Afrocentric school: A blueprint*. Universal Write Publications, LLC.

Fálàdé, F. (1998). *Ifá: The key to its understanding*. Ara Ifa Publishing.

Givens, J., & Riddick, Z. (2024). "We will just have to take it underground": A Black Studies approach to teacher education and critical professional development. *Sociology of Race and Ethnicity, 10*(4), 544–552.

Gonçalves e Silva, P. B. (2005). A new millennium research agenda in Black Education: Some points to be considered for discussion and decisions. In J. E. King (Ed.), *Black education: A transformative research and action agenda for the new millennium* (pp. 301–308). Routledge.

Hilliard III, A. G. (2011). *African power: Affirming African Indigenous socialization in the face of culture wars*. Makare Publishing Company.

Karenga, M. (1999). *Odù Ifá: The ethical teachings*. University of Sankore Press.

Kelley, R. D. G. (2025, Summer). The responsibility of intellectuals in the age of fascism and genocide. *Boston Review*, 6–25.

Kempf, A., & Dei, G. J. S. (2013). Afrocentric education in North America: An introduction. In G. J. S. Dei & A. Kempf, *New perspectives on African-centered education in Canada* (pp. 787–801). Canadian Scholars Press.

King, J. E. (2015). "Thank you for opening our minds": On praxis, transmutation, and Black Studies in teacher development. In J. E. King, *Dysconscious racism, Afrocentric praxis, and education for human freedom: Through the years I keep on toiling* (pp. 255–269). Routledge.

King, J. E. (2017). A reparatory justice curriculum for human freedom: Rewriting the story of African American dispossession and the debt owed, *Journal of African American History, 102*(2), 213–231.

King, L. J. (2019). Interpreting Black history: Toward a Black history framework for teacher education. *Urban Education, 54*(3), 368–396.

Larsen, S. (Ed.) (1996). *Zulu Shaman: Dreams, prophecies, and mysteries: Vusamazulu Credo Mutwa*. Destiny Books.

Mokam, B. (2025 , March 3). Black Studies curriculum is (defiantly) rolling out in New York City. *New York Times*. https://www.nytimes.com/2025/03/03/nyregion/black-studies-nyc-trump-executive-orders.html

Nogueira, S. G., Silva, C. B., Pereira, E. D., Chanja, M. J., & Alcântara, R. L. S. (2024). Study group in Afro-centered Psychology. *Estudos de Psicologia* (Campinas), *41*, e210183. https://doi.org/10.1590/198202 75202441e210183

Paris, P. J. (1984). *The spirituality of African peoples: The search for a common moral discourse*. Fortress Press.

Roane, J. T. (2017). *Pedagogy for the world: Black Studies in the classroom and beyond*. AAIHS. https://www.aaihs.org/pedagogy-for-the-world-black-studies-in-the-classroom-and-beyond/

Shujaa, M. J. (1994). Afrocentric transformation and parental choice in African-American independent schools. In M. J. Shujaa (Ed.), *Too much schooling, too little education: A paradox of Black life in white societies* (pp. 361–376). Africa World Press.

Shuster, K., Jeffries, H. K., & Blight, D. W. (2018). *Teaching hard history: American slavery*. Southern Poverty Law Center. https://www.splcenter.org/sites/default/files/tt_hard_history_american_slavery.pdf

Watson-Vandiver, M. J., & Wiggan, G. (2021). *The healing power of education: Afrocentric pedagogy as a tool for restoration and liberation*. Teachers College Press.

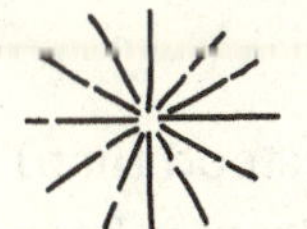

5

Preston King, Jaliyah S. Ware, and Janiyah S. Ware

What the Children We Be Lovin' Have To Say

"Eban" is an Adinkra symbol that signifies safety, security, and protection of the home (see Figure 5.1). Literally meaning "fence," it conveys the protective boundaries that safeguard the sanctuary of home. Beyond its physical meaning, Eban also serves as a metaphor for creating spaces where children feel secure enough to speak and be heard. Within such spaces, children's voices not only emerge but also flourish when they are nurtured and protected.

For too long, Black children's voices have been silenced—dismissed, overlooked, or deemed unworthy of full attention. To honor Eban is to affirm that children's words matter, that their perspectives are worthy of protection, and that their truths deserve room to resonate. In the spirit of this symbolism, we lift up the voices of three of our children and grandchildren, offering their words as reminders of what becomes possible when children are given the safety and sanctuary to speak. We hear from LaGarrett's son, Preston, and Gloria and George's granddaughters, Jaliyah and Janiyah.

In a nation so consumed with protecting white children's feelings, Black children bear their pain quietly—suffering in silence, unseen by society, and at times unnoticed even within their own families or by themselves. There are countless times in my life as a Black parent that I (Gloria) understood that I could not fully protect my children or grandchildren. I share two instances, but there are countless more. Undoubtedly, readers can think of many more.

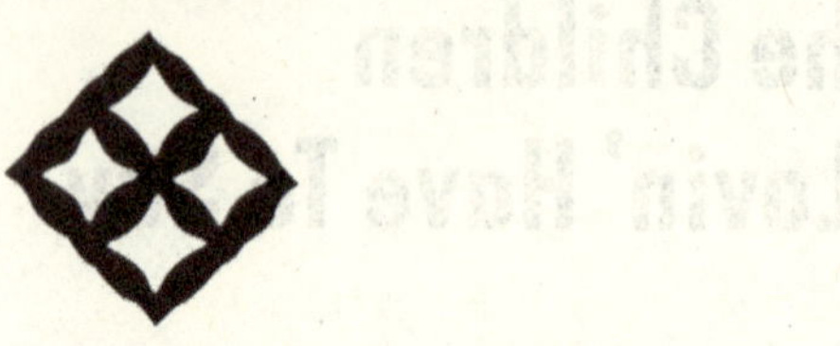

Figure 5.1. Adinkra symbol "Eban"

What Happens When Black Children Witness Ongoing Violence Against Black People?

On the day after George Floyd was murdered (May 26, 2020), I (Gloria) walked into Jaliyah's room and found her stretched across her bed with her notebook, pen, and laptop. She was weeping as she wrote (see Figure 5.2), compiling the names of Black people killed by police. Through her tears she asked me, "Why do they keep killing us?" Her anguish in that moment still pierces me. Although we talked about it, and she was beginning to realize that writing could be a tool for processing and resistance, I also felt the deep impotence that Black communities confront in the face of systemic white violence. Will learning about Black history resolve this pain? Certainly not. But it does reveal how our ancestors and elders confronted parallel injustices with agency, resilience, humanity, and collective struggle. Too often, these stories remain untold.

A second memory is of my son, Jonathan, when he was in third or fourth grade. One afternoon he came home shaken and fearful, explaining that he had learned about the white terrorist group, the Ku Klux Klan, which had killed—and still kills—Black people. We talked about how Black communities have always resisted and fought back, but I could see that he remained frightened and uncertain. Though we

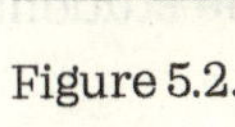

Figure 5.2.

have intergenerationally educated our children and grand-children about Black history, they spend enormous amounts of time in school and society hearing and seeing the opposite of what we teach. We call on Black communities to buffer our children with Black history in afterschool, Saturday/Sunday schools, night schools, etc.

Other chapters in this book highlight affirmative and agentic stories, but these moments remind us of the urgency. Our children encounter the terror of anti-Black violence early, and it is our responsibility to give them not only the truth, but also the examples of how our people have responded with strength and vision. Preston, Jaliyah, and Janiyah responded to three questions.

1. In what ways do/did you feel loved as a Black child?

2. Talk about love, or lack of love, in school.

3. What advice do you offer about loving Black children?

We begin with Preston's story. Jaliyah and Janiyah are twins and are now sophomores in college.

Preston King—Founder of the First Black Student Union in His Middle School

Preston King is a freshman student-athlete in a high school in New York state. In 2024, he created the first Black Student Union (BSU) at a middle school in the school district. The idea came about when he heard of the BSU at the high school and responded to a school survey asking students the most press-ing concerns at the school. Out of 500 plus students, 300 plus students said that the racial climate and racism (anti-Black-ness) was the biggest concern at the school. The school is 80% white. Black students were less than 5% of the student population.

Preston complained about racism at the school throughout his 3 years. Incidents involved white male students' use of the N-word and other racial stereotypes towards Black students (i.e., calling Black students *monkey*). Black students were disciplined more than their white counterparts, and many believed that their teachers were prejudiced against them. A sign of a larger and anti-Black issue at the school was at the end of the school award ceremony. No Black or Brown students received awards, including Preston, who was lauded for his leadership with young students and the BSU in private but did not receive any of the school's three leadership awards.

The BSU served as a space where students, especially students of color, at the school could come and talk about things that concerned them. Also, he wanted a space where the students could just be themselves and love each other. The BSU held six meetings with an average attendance between 14 and 20 students. All meetings took place before school.

In what ways do/did you feel loved as a Black child?

I feel loved as a Black child now because of my family supporting me and social media having different communities and places that I can express myself as a loved Black child.

Talk about love, or lack of love, in school.

In school, sometimes I do feel a little bit like an outsider, but then I remember that my many friends can help me through anything, internal or external.

What advice do you offer about loving Black children?

Some advice I can give to loving Black children is to embrace your differences, because that's what makes you unique in special ways.

Janiyah Ware

In what ways do/did you feel loved as a Black child?

Growing up, I felt most loved as a Black child in my household. It was my safe place . . . being able to have a family that understands the beauty of our skin.

Talk about love, or lack of love, in school.

When it came around for me to start going to a public school, I started off in a white school so I felt more uncomfortable and not as confident because of how much I stood out. Due to me being dark skinned, made it worse. I was talked about and made fun of. This made me go into a phase where I didn't want to be Black. Although my family didn't tolerate my not wanting to be Black and never let me forget how important it is just to be Black and that's what helped me learn how to love my skin.

What advice do you offer about loving Black children?

My advice to all Black children is no matter where you are and how light or dark your melanin may be, you're beautiful, and never let anyone make you feel differently; being Black is a blessing.

Jaliyah Ware

In what ways do/did you feel loved as a Black child?

I felt loved by my family mostly because they always made sure that I knew where I came from and that it wasn't anything to be ashamed of—even though that's how it was perceived by my school or textbooks. My family also made sure I had everything and more—educationally, financially, and emotionally.

Talk about love, or lack of love, in school.

Like I said previously, there is love in school until you get older and realize there wasn't any real love from the educational system but really only from friends and teachers if you're lucky. This may be the experience I had because I was one of 10 Black students in my school. But looking back being older, I'm not sure if that is the only issue either.

What advice do you offer about loving Black children?
Black children need love from a loving person. You can't fake love. Making sure Black youth know how powerful and significant they are and how much stems from their ancestral roots.

I also think it's very important to teach what they teach in school but also balance it out with good things. As a child hearing only about what we went through, from the people who did it to our ancestors and also hearing THEIR sides of OUR story confuses us. I would think maybe white people had more power because why would my people just sit there for so long—for so many years. But when I got home and my grandparents taught me [that] we fought, and even before we had to fight, we had so much more than what they said we did before we were taken and snatched from our land.

What Adults Can Support Black Children

The pain of being marginalized and picked on are evident in Preston's, Janiyah's, and Jaliyah's responses. But so is the power of Black love to overcome the pain that the world hurls their way. Themes from their responses reflect the importance of family and friends in Pro-Black identity development. None of them mentioned adult support in integrated schools (teachers, please heed the call!). Where is the love? None of the children talked about love—only harm. Schools have a problem loving Black children, and the three questions could serve as an "audit" for those serious about loving Black children.

We suggest that these three questions be asked of Black children. We value these questions because they affirm that Black children are loved, while also inviting them to reflect on this truth and to hold it close as armor against the endemic adversities of anti-Blackness.

A second critical step is to encourage children to act against anti-Blackness and to nurture Pro-Blackness. These actions may be large or small and will vary depending on the context, but they are all meaningful. Just as important, adults must stand with children and youth—partnering with them to advance Pro-Black policies and programs. If you truly love Black children (and we know you do), then show up, speak out, and advocate alongside them.

An unspoken question that runs through this chapter is: *What will you do to recognize and respond to Black children's pain?* We are not naïve enough to believe that such pain can be erased entirely in an anti-Black world. Yet we must do more than offer bandages for their deep wounds while sending them back into the white-centered battlegrounds we call schools. Our charge is to affirm Black children's worth, amplify their voices, and walk with them as they transform pain into power, creating new possibilities for freedom, joy, and collective healing.

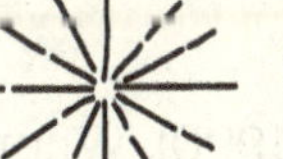

Jarvais J. Jackson, Saudah N. Collins, Janice Baines, and Valente' Gibson

Say It Loud—I'm Black and I'm Proud: Beauty, Brilliance, and Belonging in Our Homes, Classrooms, and Communities

Uh! Your bad self!
Say it loud! I'm black and I'm proud
Say it louder! I'm black and I'm proud
Look a-here!
Some people say we got a lot of malice, some say it's a lotta nerve
But I say we won't quit movin' until we get what we deserve
We've been 'buked and we've been scorned
We've been treated bad, talked about as sure as you're born
But just as sure as it take two eyes to make a pair, huh!
Brother we can't quit until we get our share

—Brown (1969)

James Brown's iconic song "I'm Black and I'm Proud" provides a proclamation that we as Black people should instill in ourselves and our children as we navigate through any space. Honoring and embracing our Blackness is something that we have not often been taught to do. Dating back to 1933, Carter G. Woodson, known as the Father of Black History, asserted Black people are often taught to hate everything

Black and love everything white (Woodson, 1933/1990). When it comes to places such as schools, we have been taught to hide our Blackness through code-switching and other respectability politics. Black people have been taught not to "talk Black" and to suppress other Black cultural expressions. None of this is healthy for us as Black people.

This chapter shares ways that love of Blackness can be celebrated at home and in our communities. Our hope is that Blackness becomes such a strong force in our children that they freely express themselves at school. We share practices that we use in our classrooms as elementary school teachers. Throughout the year, we find ways to teach the seven principles of Kwanzaa (*Nguzo Saba* in Swahili):

- *Umoja*—unity

- *Kujichagulia*—self-determination

- *Ujima*— collective work and responsibility

- *Ujamaa*—cooperative economics

- *Nia*—purpose

- *Kuumba*—creativity

- *Imani*—faith

These seven principles provide a foundational value system that Black children, families, and communities can live by. The learning examples that we share can also be done in Black homes and communities. Some activities cover more than one principle.

Umoja (Unity) and Nia (Purpose)

Fostering unity (togetherness) takes time and a common purpose. Consider focusing on issues that are greater than any one individual. This takes us back to the African principles of communalism rather than individualism. In our classrooms, we use Adinkra symbols from the Akan people in Ghana and Cote D'Ivoire. As students grow to know each other and build a sense of community, we use the Adinkra symbol *nkonsonkonson* (Figure 6.1) as a visual reminder as students think about its chain link.

Figure 6.1. The Adinkra symbol nkonsonkonson
Source: http://www.adinkra.org/htmls/adinkra/nkon.htm

We focus on strengthening bonds by encouraging solidarity, attitudes toward justice, and community in classrooms, schools, homes, and communities. We examine our historical and contemporary connections as Black people through song, dance, visual art, storytelling, and literature studies. Through these activities, our students become more unified and prouder.

Music. Music can play a vital role in connecting to students. We suggest using positive music often to counter negative messages about Black people. In our experiences, most students love music, and they usually learn lyrics to music quite quickly. Using this interest, we often use music in our classrooms to start a dialogue around topics or to share a specific message. Examples of the types of songs used and their particular themes can be found in Table 6.1.

An example using music to engage children and youth in conversations about faith (imani) and self-determination (kujichagulia) can be seen in Baltimore's Cardinal Shehan

Table 6.1. Music to Teach Unity and Faith

Title	Artist	Theme
"Tomorrow"	Tevin Campbell (Johnson & Johnson, 1976)	Hope
"Strength, Courage, Wisdom"	India Arie (Simpson, 2000)	Empowerment
"Love's in Need of Love Today"	Stevie Wonder (1976)	Love vs. Hate
"Wake Up Everybody"	John Legend (2010)	Take action
"Black Butterfly"	Deniece Williams (Mann & Well, 1984)	Perseverance
"My Power"	Beyoncé (Ggulu et al., 2019)	Strength
"A Change is Gonna Come"	Sam Cooke (1964)	Triumph
"Glory"	John Legend (Stephens et al., 2014)	Civil Rights

School's performance of Andra Day's "Rise Up" (see WJZ, 2017). We have used the video during morning gatherings to convey the message about standing up in the pursuit of justice. For some students, the song verbalizes feelings they are experiencing as they are exposed to racism through personal experiences and stories they see on the news. For many students, this is a message of hope. After watching the video, we engage students in discussions about how they can work together as a unified force (umoja—unity) to stand up against injustices in their communities and in society.

Music can also be a way to affirm the beauty of Black people. For example, Beyoncé's (2019) "Brown Skin Girl" opens up with

Brown skin girl
Your skin just like pearls
The best thing in the world
never trade you for anybody else

This song serves as a message that Black girls are beautiful and priceless. They often do not hear this in school or in society. Other songs, such as Nas's (2002) "I Can," ignites students' dreams and ambitions reminding them that they can be whatever they put their minds to be (kujichagulia—self-determination). Use these songs, and others, to constantly remind our Black children they are beautiful, powerful, and valuable. Songs like these can be played in the car on the way to school or at home while everyone is getting dressed. Songs can be anthems proclaiming our purpose (nia).

Kujichagulia (Self-Determination)

In our classes, we explore the principle of self-determination in multiple ways gleaning knowledge from many past and present role models throughout the African Diaspora, such as the widely known story of Rosa Parks to the not-so-well-known story of Sarah Mae Flemming from South Carolina who also refused to sit in the back of a bus. We teach children that it is important to reclaim the ability to define and speak for ourselves. Students learn that affirming messages from their teachers, peers, songs, historical accounts, and literature can help them redefine what it means to be Black and proud. We engage students in dialogue and study about Black hair texture, style, skin tone, language, interactional styles, and clothing selections throughout the year. Ongoing efforts like this are necessary to help Black children and youth transform an internalized Black people's self-determination (kujichagulia). In the following, we provide additional suggestions for exploring the principle of kujichagulia (self-determination).

Contemporary Role Models. Contemporary role models often give relatable examples of how students can develop self-determination. In one of our classes, students learned about the experiences of Kheris Rogers, a young girl tormented by her classmates because of her dark brown skin.

With her family's support, she countered the negative, hateful experience with bold positive messaging of self-love. Kheris started a clothing company with the slogan "Flexin' in My Complexion," which means being proud of one's complexion (*CBS This Morning*, 2018). When Black children learn to value all shades of Blackness, it counters European standards of beauty.

Connecting their interest in sports, we have conversations about athletes and self-determination that allowed them to reach their success. For example, A'ja Wilson, a University of South Carolina women's basketball player, worked through her dyslexia to be a nationally acclaimed professional. At home, engage children in conversations about contemporary role models. Importantly, remember that role models may be family and community members.

Positive Literature. The use of affirming literature can give birth to explorations of Black people naming ourselves and our values and contributions. Through the use of positive literature, children can be inspired by seeing themselves in culturally affirming ways. Remember, *schools often do not include ongoing positive literature about Black people.*

Table 6.2 provides a list of books with affirming messages that would be appropriate for use by children ages 3 through 12. Video read-alouds are also an option and can be found online by doing a Google search. Many more examples can be found on websites like this one: https://aalbc.com/books/children.php.

Visual Art. As we continue to build positive self-identity with literature, affirmations, and music, student engagement and input are vital. At the start of the year, we ask students to introduce themselves and tell their classmates about themselves. Using mirrors to assist with this exploration, students are asked to look at their facial features and then illustrate what they see. These illustrations then become self-portraits.

Table 6.2. Positive Books For Children Ages 3–12

Title	Author	Theme
Ages 3–8		
I Am Enough (Byers, 2018)	Grace Byers	Empowerment
I Am Every Good Thing (Barnes, 2020)	Derrick Barnes	Empowerment
What if . . . ? (Berger, 2018)	Samantha Berger	Inspiration
Hair Love (Cherry, 2019)	Matthew A. Cherry	Uplifting
The Day You Begin (Woodson, 2019)	Jacqueline Woodson	Encouragement
Ages 9–12		
Crown: An Ode to the Fresh Cut (Barnes, 2017)	Derrick Barnes	Empowerment
One Crazy Summer (Williams-Garcia, 2010)	Rita Williams-Garcia	Uplifting
The Parker Inheritance (Johnson 2018)	Varian Johnson	Inspiration
Preaching To The Chickens: The Story of Young (Asim, 2016)	Jabari Asim	Encouragement
The Undefeated (Alexander, 2019)	Kwame Alexander	Resistance

To emphasize the classroom community, the self-portraits are later displayed as art around the classroom. Every day, the students walk in and see themselves. See examples in Figure 6.2.

Figure 6.2. Examples of Students' Self-Portraits

Ujima (Collective Work and Responsibility)

Cultivating a unified learning community that reflects the importance of togetherness and responsibility is important to the foundation of student learning and success. As teachers, we acknowledge that without collective work and struggle, progress and liberation are impossible. We share lessons learned that families and community members can use to explore the principle of Ujima.

Maintain a Focus on "We," Not "I." We use the Adinkra symbol *boa me na me mmoa wo* (Figure 6.3) to focus on commitment, interdependence, cooperation, and the common good. At home and in the community, the focus should not be on the individual. Rather, emphasis should be on the collective with members working together to solve problems and share in the benefits of family or group efforts. These efforts should be rooted in honoring African traditions and practices, such as those shared in Chapter 10. Working collectively brings together knowledge, expertise, strength, and purpose and can foster a greater sense of ownership and pride in one's community.

Figure 6.3. The Adinkra symbol boa me na me mmoa wo. Family time. *Source:* http://www.adinkra.org/htmls/adinkra/boame.htm

If you want to go alone, go fast. If you want to go far, go together.

This African proverb expresses the importance of working together as a collective instead of focusing only on self-achievement. In our classrooms, we create a family atmosphere that allows students to succeed, struggle, and grow collectively. A family is not always blood-related. A family can be people who accept us for who we are and who are willing to support us in our life journeys. Family time is used to celebrate victories or to work through obstacles that have come up. The following suggestions emphasize the importance of togetherness and responsibility for families and communities:

- Take time to talk—Dedicate time to talk without distractions (e.g., electronics, television).

- Record family stories—Build family histories by recording the stories and memoirs of family members and community members (i.e., time spent at a local store or restaurant, barbershop or beauty salon, or time spent doing family traditions such as holidays or Sunday dinners).

- Community and family timelines—Children can interview family members and make an illustrated timeline of the most important family events and memories.

- Name storybook—Children can interview family members and create a family name storybook (e.g., Where did I get my name from? Who helped name me?).

Conclusion

While there is no one way to reach the ultimate goal of embracing Black beauty and brilliance, we hope that these examples provide starting points and ideas to use. Of course, these examples should be tailored to the needs of families, classrooms, and community settings. Importantly, we advise not avoiding conversations on what it means to be Black and proud and to love Blackness.

References

Alexander, K. (2019). *The undefeated*. Houghton Mifflin Harcourt.

Asim, J. (2016). *Preaching to the chickens: The story of Young*. Nancy Paulsen Books.

Barnes, D. (2017). *Crown: The ode to the fresh cut*. Agate Bolden.

Barnes, D. (2020). *I am every good thing*. Nancy Paulsen Books.

Berger, S. (2018). *What if* . . . Little, Brown Books for Young Readers.

Beyoncé. (2019). Brown skin girl [Song]. On *The lion king: The gift* [Album] Parkwood Entertainment/Columbia Records.

Brown, J. (1969). Say it loud – I'm Black and I'm proud [Song]. On *Say it loud – I'm Black and I'm proud* [Album]. UMG.

Byers, G. (2018). *I am enough*. Balzer & Bray.

CBS This Morning. (2018, July 31). *Flexin' in my complexion: 11-year-old transforms bullying experience into success* [Video]. YouTube. https://www.youtube.com/watch?v=pKa44qL_8Zs

Cherry, M. A. (2019). *Hair love*. Kokila.

Cooke, S. (1964). A change is gonna come [Song]. On *Ain't That Good News* [Album]. RCA Victor.

Gqulu, B. B., Twisha, S., Charles, A. C., & Gwala, L. (2019). Strength [Song]. On *The lion king: The gift* [Album]. Parkwood Entertainment/Columbia Records.

Johnson, G., & Johnson, L. (1976). Tomorrow (a better you, better me) [Song]. On *Look out for #1* [Album]. A & M Records.

Johnson, V. (2018). *The Parker inheritance*. Arthur A. Levine Books.

Legend, J. (2010). Wake up! [Song]. On *The roots* [Album]. GOOD/Columbia.

Mann, B., & Well, C. (1984). Black butterfly [Song]. On *Let's hear it for the boys* [Album]. Columbia.

Nas. (2002). I can [Song]. On *God's son* [Album]. Sony.

Simpson, I. A. (2000). Strength, courage, & wisdom [Song]. On *Bamboozled* [Album]. Warner Chappell Music.

Stephens, J., Lynn, L., & Smith, C. (2014). Glory [Song]. On *Selma soundtrack* [Album]. ARTium/Def Jam/Columbia.

Williams-Garcia, R. (2010). *One crazy summer*. HarperCollins.

WJZ. (2017, October 12). *Students from Baltimore's Cardinal Shehan School sing "Rise Up"* [Video]. YouTube. https://www.youtube.com/watch?v=IEGEovFX534

Wonder, S. (1976). Love's in need of love today [Song]. On *Songs in the key of life* [Album]. Tamla/Motown.

Woodson, C. G. (1990). *The mis-education of the Negro*. Africa World Press. (Original work published 1933)

Woodson, J. (2019). *The day you begin*. Penguin Young Readers Group.

7

Shaquetta Moultrie, Antoinette Gibson,
and Julia Dawson

Great Rising: Activities to Inspire Black Teens and Youth[1]

Black Girl Magic Project—Shaquetta Moultrie

Michelle Obama. Beyoncé. Simone Biles. Rihanna. This is a concise list of successful Black women. I could write a book outlining their accomplishments. Michelle Obama, first lady and woman of the millennium (as far as we are concerned)—children, teens, and adults admire her. Beyoncé has a following so huge that when she performed at the Super Bowl, people on social media said there was a football game at the "Beyoncé concert." Simone Biles's talent and determination have made her a top gymnast globally, winning four Olympic gold medals. Rihanna, a young talent from Barbados, is the world's wealthiest female singer, owning both makeup and lingerie lines, Fenty and Savage, respectively. She also started the Clara Lionel Foundation to fund education projects and health and emergency response following disasters worldwide.

But you don't have to be famous to possess "Black Girl Magic." All Black women have it. I'm not saying that magic

---

1   Activities in this chapter are focused on Black youth ages 11 to 16, but youth of different ages may also enjoy them.

is not in everyone, but that's just not my current focus. The wonders and beauty of Black and Brown women have been suppressed, covered up, even buried. Children are vulnerable and impressionable. Popular social media, television, magazine images, and so on shape how beauty is defined in society. In modern U.S. history, that definition did not include dark skin, kinky-curly hair, full lips, and full, curvy figures. Instead, these images show light, bright, damn-near white skin, long silky hair, and slim, straight-figured women with thin lips covered in red lipstick.

Chimamanda Adichie, a Nigerian American author, speaks about the dangers of a single story about any group of people and how this creates stereotypes. How a story is told, who tells it, the audience, and how often it's said can make that story dangerous. In the case of stories about the beauty or lack thereof, in Black women—they've been told so much, for so long, by so many people, to so many people—that it's embedded in our Black and Brown girls' psyches. They don't believe they are supermodel pretty.

C'mon, how many of our daughters aspire to be dark-skinned sisters like Maria Borges, Nyakim Gatwech, or Alek Wek? We must teach our daughters, sisters, nieces, and cousins about Black Girl Magic because society won't. Society shares a single story. Until we become the authors, coming from different perspectives, Black girls will believe the tale that deflects their beauty and diminishes their pride.

Let me tell you a story. It starts with a small girl who was her mother's firstborn and the second born to her father. She and her sister were like ebony and ivory. She was a smooth chocolate brown; her sister was often asked if she was "mixed with white." The ebony daughter, at the young age of 5, despised her complexion. When she purchased dolls, she wanted the "tan"-colored toy. One day, her mother asked, "Why don't you like darker dolls?" Her daughter called them "ugly." Immediately, the mother knew they needed to have a longer talk. In the conversation that followed, she learned that her daughter wanted lighter skin and freckles. She wanted to look more like her sister because everyone called her sister "pretty." This was heartbreaking for her mother to hear. Her mother knew something had to be done, but she was confused, filled with questions: "When did this configuration in the Brown girl's brain happen?" How and why did it happen?"

The young girl in this story is my daughter. Had I not sat down with her after that store visit, I would never have known that she didn't feel worthy in her own skin. We live in a technological age where social media largely idolizes the *opposite* of Brown girls, and they feel this. This is why we must become a narrator in our girls' lives. We have to speak to the profound beauty in them—expose them to something other than the single story they're told. With that in mind, I propose the following activities, which I have titled **The Black Girl Magic Project**. (Boys may also do them.)

Activity 1: The Danger of a Single Story

Have children watch the 19-minute TED Talk on YouTube *The Danger of a Single Story* with Chimamanda Ngozi Adichie (https://www.ted.com/talks/chimamanda_ngozi_adichie_the_danger_of_a_single_story?language=en). Adichie speaks on how society sees and hears one side of a story, and this story shapes and defines what is. Adichie is from Nigeria, West Africa. Before starting the video, ask children what they know about Africa (i.e., What is it like? How do the people look? How do they live?). After the video, ask them if they still believe everything they thought before. Why or why not? Have them think about and discuss how society has labeled Black people. Using this information, let the child(ren) create a word collage on stereotypes about Black people. Discuss where they got this story and how it could be dangerous to youth who believe it. Then have children create a collage depicting a new story—one with positive words describing Black people. Finally, engage in dialogue about why it's important for Black people to grow and learn more about themselves and where our ancestors come from.

Activity 2: Introduction to Black Girl Magic

Ask the child(ren) what they know about the Black Girl Magic movement. After this discussion, have them look up the Black Girl Magic movement to learn more information, such as the founder, what it means, and why it began. Finally, have them write a poem about what Black Girl Magic means to them (see http://www.blackgirlmagicmag.com/about-1).

Activity 3: Shades of Magic

In this activity, have the child(ren) look through Black publications to find various Black women (or teens or children) with success stories. Suggested magazines include *Essence, Ebony, Black Beauty, PRIDE*, and *Today's Black Woman*. Once they find the pictures, they will create a poster with the women's names and achievements. This activity exposes children to the diverse looks and shades of Black women to instill in them that Black is beautiful. It will also allow them to see diversity in the types of successes Black women have. You don't have to be a movie star or singer to be successful. You can be an author, teacher, parent, politician, veterinarian, entrepreneur, and a thousand other possibilities. Black Girl Magic flows in many different ways.

Activity 4: Where They Get That From?

In this activity, children research how many things in popular culture are rooted in Africa. They can consider hair, music, and dance for starters. For example, children will find that braids existed in ancient Africa, are common in contemporary Africa, and are now extremely popular in the United States. This activity aims to shift the mindset of the single story and show that there are many African cultures, not just one, and they've influenced African Americans since our ancestors first came to the United States.

Activity 5: You Got That Black Girl Magic

In this activity, the children will think about women in their lives and list Black Girl Magic attributes they possess. This activity aims to teach our youth about lifting each other up rather than tearing each other down, understanding that beauty comes in many different shapes, forms, and fashions. It also emphasizes learning about past generations.

Activity 6: I Got That Black Girl Magic—The Beauty in YOU

In this final activity, children will create an autobiography. They will discuss their own personal success stories. Whether they're good at writing, drawing, painting, singing…whatever! The goal is to highlight their own beauty. This can be completed by creating a PowerPoint presentation or writing a book or short story. Invite them to include pictures of themselves with captions. Encourage them to share their stories.

Tearing down the boundaries that define beauty and building up Black girls' confidence is a necessity. Cashawn Thompson said she started the Black Girl Magic movement to honor girls and women relatives and friends that were doing things so incredible that it seemed magical to her (Black Girl Magic, 2020). Her movement blew up on social media. This activity aims to help young girls everywhere recognize themselves and the magical things they do that go unnoticed every day.

Black Malehood and Freedom—Antoinette Gibson

After my third year as a teacher, I had an alarming discovery. I noticed that African American males were not being stimulated academically. I also saw how many Black male students were receiving special education services. I realized that African American males are more engaged during kinesthetic, or tactile, learning activities. Therefore, I recommend inviting Black male teens to move, draw, dance, sing, or express themselves in other ways—physically and orally.

One way adults can be forces of healing in Black boys' lives is by making nonjudgmental spaces for them to fully express themselves. Five such activities are offered next.

Activity 1: Bruh Genius

Sample prompts such as the following ones can help Black boys learn and express themselves:

- What are your learning preferences?

- What do you like and not like about school based on your experiences so far?

- Describe what you already know about the history and art forms created by African Americans from the 1600s to now.

Engage the young men in discussion about their answers. Share African traditions of storytelling and oral art forms and discuss the importance of Black people expressing ourselves. Here's one resource: "The Legacy of Storytelling in African-American History" from *CBS This Morning* (https://www.youtube.com/watch?v=I5hth0VvSyA).

Activity 2: Lyrical Swagger

Play clean versions of Lil Baby's "The Bigger Picture" (https://www.youtube.com/watch?v=v7GrlW3y_r0) and Trey Songz's "2020 Riots: How Many Times?" (https://www.youtube.com/watch?v=wWz1LI1aF-A). Talk with the teens about injustice and how these Black male artists use intellectual and creative oral communication skills to speak persuasively about it.

Activity 3: Research Time

Tell youth you're now going to jump from 2020, back through U.S. history to 1961 through 1974. Help them create a timeline that displays at least four to six historical events of the Black Freedom Movement between 1961 and 1974. Here are some resources:

- Zinn Education Project (Black nationalist, People's Movement): https://www.zinnedproject.org/materials/?s=black+nationalist&cond[0]=period_str:1961

- Stanford University. The Martin Luther King, Jr. Research and Education Institute: https://kinginstitute.stanford.edu/encyclopedia/black-nationalism

Next, let youth do a Google search and find short, informative, accurate, and engaging videos from or about the 1961–1974 period for the state you live in. The videos should go along with the timeline events.

Activity 4: Image Search

Ask youth to do a Google search for three to five pictures of the civil rights/Black nationalist movements between 1961 and 1974. Ask them to write the date and describe what different images show. Talk about the answers with your child, or have them draw and fill out the chart in Table 7.1 for each picture.

Table 7.1. Image Search

Picture and date picture was taken	What story does the picture tell? What does it mean? Why does it matter?
	Tell: Mean: Matter:

Activity 5: Say It Loud, Black, and Proud

Youth will use background knowledge from their research, timeline, videos, and pictures to create a story about the history they researched. They'll compare the history to their own lives today as young Black male teens in the United States. They can use Lil Baby's and Trey Songz's songs as models. The teens then turn their stories into a poem, rap, song, essay, speech, poster, or another format that they choose. Invite the teens to share their work with you at family or other events.

Cherishing Black Children's Names—Julia Dawson

The Color Purple author Alice Walker, boxer Muhammad Ali, and the Muslim minister and activist Malcolm X—all of them examined their names. Alice Walker chose to keep her birth name. Ali and Malcolm X changed theirs. These are three examples of *millions* of messengers of Black love and power.

The power to name holds within it many other powers. The What's in MY Name project invites Black teens to research the stories of their names to reclaim or cherish the African and African American legacies alive in them. Before starting, read through the activities yourself to better guide your teen.

Activity 1: My Blackness. My Name: Where I Am Right Now

Ask these questions. Take notes or record children's answers as a family keepsake.

1. Do you call yourself Black? Why or why not?

2. What does the word *Black*, as in Black people, mean to you?

3. What do you know about your full name? How do you feel about it?

Invite the child to share out loud and/or create a drawing, poem, or song using supplies like paint and paper or a cellphone app such as TikTok.

Activity 2: Malcolm X and "Slave Names"

Listen to a short clip from one famous, often misrepresented, Black American: the Muslim minister, activist, and pan-Africanist Malcolm X. The clip shows a little about him, but there's *much* more to learn!

Ask your child what they already know about him. Use *BLACKPAST, Malcolm X (1925-1965)* (https://www.blackpast. org/african-american-history/x-malcolm-1925-1965/) to learn more. If your teen labels him "hateful," discuss how and why people like Malcolm X have been misrepresented. This is a chance to focus on how he showed Black love and power. Have children watch *Malcolm X: Slave Names* (https://www. youtube.com/watch?v=MBtZwVioc_I&t=3s&pbjreload=101). After listening, ask children to answer the questions on paper and/or discuss it together:

1. List two main ideas Malcolm X makes in this clip.

2. What is Malcolm X saying about African Americans' last names?

3. Would you ever want to change your name? Why or why not?

Activity 3: Naming Traditions From Different African Groups

Read with your teen *This Is How Traditional Naming Ceremonies Are Performed Across the African Diaspora* (Malik, 2018). Read this resource over 2 days. Consider focusing on the parts in Table 7.2. Discuss, audio record, or invite your teen to write answers.

Table 7.2. Questions About African Names and Naming Ceremonies

Describe three details of the Edo naming ceremony. What are examples of Edo names?	
What do the Yoruba people believe about the meaning of a child's name? What are at least two reasons the naming ceremony is so important?	
When must the Akan naming ceremony occur? How is water used in the ceremony? What are examples of Akan names?	

Activity 4: "Know Thyself"

Now your child will research her/his name!

1. Write three to six interview questions together.

2. Decide who to interview. Have them call those relatives/friends.

3. Video, audio record, or listen and take notes during the interview(s).

4. Invite the teen to use the interview(s) to create a speech, poem, rap, dance, painting, collage using PowerPoint, a WordPress webpage, or an actual poster all about their name. It can include pictures and words about their name's meaning and history, plus how it connects to African and African American traditions. Figure 7.1 is one example.

After the project, ask, "Have your views about who you are or Black people and history changed? If yes, how?" To share your experiences, use this link: https://docs.google.

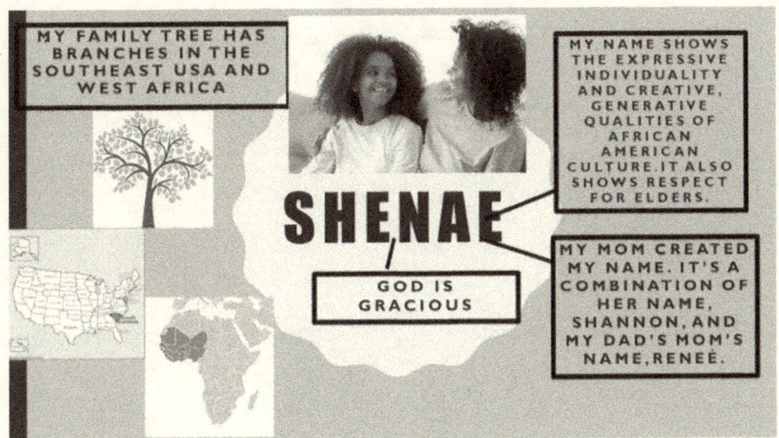

Figure 7.1. Sample of Name Research Activity

com/forms/d/e/1FAIpQLSf5FBPMOxEvmd0T2ePC7n9Uquc 4j9H6nJkYLBHoo96-GTOS4A/viewform.

References

Black Girl Magic. (2020). *Black girls are magic. The movement.* https://www. godaddy.com/garage/how-one-woman-started-a-movement-with-blackgirlmagic/

Malik, A. (2018). *This is how traditional naming ceremonies are performed across the African Diaspora.* The Pan-African Alliance. https:// www.panafricanalliance.com/african-renaming-ceremonies/

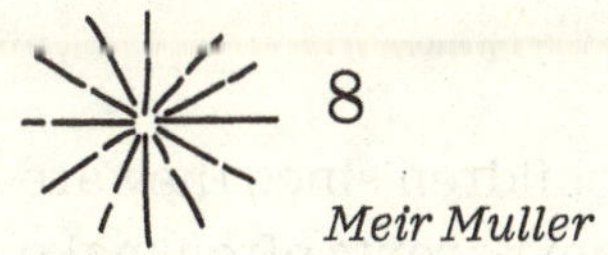

8

Meir Muller

Preparing Black Children to Identify and Confront Racism in Books, Media, and Other Texts: Critical Questions

This chapter offers questions to empower Black children to identify and confront messages that distort or omit information about African and African American history, people, and communities. These critical questions are suited for children of all ages. They can examine books, advertisements, music, television, movies, and other media content for racially discriminating language, illustrations, and story lines. Critical questions are one way that Black adults can help buffer Black children from anti-Black racism.

What Black Children Are Learning About Themselves

The Adinkra symbol *mate masie* (pronounced Mah-ti Mah-see-eh) means "What I hear, I keep" (Figure 8.1), symbolizes knowledge, wisdom, and the prudence of taking into consideration what another person has shared in our journey to gain information, knowledge, and understanding. At the same time, taken literally, the symbol implies that what people are told (and hear) can have a deep, long-lasting influence on them. This is particularly true of children since they are impressionable. While comments from parents often make strong impressions on children, so do messages in books, movies, television, music, conversations, and other texts. All these influences can impact children's perceptions of themselves.

Figure 8.1. Adinkra symbol mate masie, "What I hear, I keep," a symbol of wisdom, knowledge, and prudence.
Source: http://www.adinkra.org/htmls/adinkra/mate.htm

Black families often shine a light on children's brilliance. However, when children go to school, they are likely to see negative portrayals of Black people and their potential. Additionally, research shows that Black children are regularly over-referred to special education, under-referred to gifted programs, and unfairly disciplined. Black history, language, and culture are often omitted or misrepresented in school curricula. As a matter of fact, Black children often first see themselves represented in school textbooks as people who are enslaved and then not again till the limited appearance of very incomplete descriptions of a few well-known (dead) Black people such as Dr. Martin Luther King Jr., Harriet Tubman, Rosa Parks, and others. The long history of African people that spans thousands of years is often not covered in school. These negative and omitted examples of Black experiences can cause personal, psychological, and spiritual injuries to children.

What Can Be Done to Keep Black Children's Self-Esteem Intact?

First, it is essential to know that Black people have always been actively working on letting children know that they are "Young, Gifted, and Black" and to keep "their souls intact." For example, African American communities have published books describing Black brilliance, purchased and shared positive Black books with their children, produced radio and television programs to counter negative racial messages, organized public protests, and led legal challenges to improve their community schools.

Second, children have historically been part of many of these efforts. In the 1920s, Black children had been featured in publications that countered racist issues (e.g., W. E. B. Du Bois & Fauset's (1920–1921) *Brownies' Book*; Shackelford's (1944) *My Happy Days*; and Tarry and Ets's (1946) *My Dog Rinty*). Black children have been actors on groundbreaking television programs that called out systemic racism. An early example is the 1960s' *Inside Bed-Stuy*, in which Black children chanted, "What has America done for me? Nothing, but made me a zombie—I don't know who I am!" (Cole, 2003, "From Belafonte to Black Power"). Perhaps the most famous example of children protesting is the Children's Crusade in Birmingham, Alabama, during May 1963. During this time, thousands of African American children walked out of school and marched for civil rights.

Today, we once again see Black children confronting injustice as they march in #BlackLivesMatter protests and produce their own antiracist content on social media. This chapter's critical questions will help Black children push back against words and texts that try to negatively depict or misrepresent their life experiences and culture.

Black Children Are Aware of Injustices

Every parent knows that children ask questions at a relentless pace. These questions often show children's innate ability to discern fairness, injustice, and power. For example, children may ask, "Why does my friend have a later bedtime than me?" or "Why does my brother get to pick what game we play?" Children also address more weighty issues such as "Why is COVID-19 affecting more Black people?" and "Why do police kill unarmed Black people?" The children's keen understanding of fairness, justice, and inequity is the basis for critical questions.

Critical Questions That Can Help Discuss Racism With Children and Youth

Black children and youth need to know that they can question what they read, see, and hear. When children ask critical questions, they embody the Adinkra symbol, mate masie, a symbol of wisdom, knowledge, and good judgment. As Black children learn the art of taking critical stances, they understand that they do not have to agree with what is written in books or shown in the media and the world about Black people. Children and youth become detectives in noticing whose voices are prioritized, minimized, or overlooked. Following are sample questions and prompts that can help children recognize racism and other types of injustices in books, television, music, video games, movies, social media, different types of texts, and life:

- Are Black people included in this text? Why or why not?

- Do you see anything unfair to Black people? Tell me more about this.

- Who or what is shown as necessary? How was the message of importance conveyed?

- Are Black people left out or shown as unimportant? How was this message conveyed?

- Can this message be hurtful or unfair to Black people? Why?

- How does the text make you feel? Why?

- What can you do to improve this issue?

At first, adults might need to lead children through the questions as they look critically at advertisements, books, and media. Eventually, children can use these questions as a lens through which they process everyday interactions.

What Are Advertisements Selling?

The American Academy of Pediatrics reports that children see upward of 40,000 advertisements a year (American Psychological Association, 2004). We know that many of these contain images and words that can damage African American children's self-image—even if they are not aware of it. Encouraging children to use critical questions can transform passive or subconscious acceptance of these messages to active rejection and confrontation.

In addition to advertisements selling the products they feature, they also can sell harmful racist messages. The following three examples show how critical questions can be used to confront detrimental and dangerous advertisements.

1. In a Dove body wash advertisement, a Black woman pulls a shirt over her head and emerges as a white woman (Chan, 2017). Asking children if they see anything unfair and who is shown as important can help

children detect if the ad is suggesting that a soap that "gets you whiter" is glorifying white people. Asking children who is left out or shown as unimportant or who might find this image to be hurtful or unfair can help children identify that this advertisement diminishes Black people's dignity and worth.

2. A similar example is an advertisement for Gap Kids in which the elbow of a tall white child rests on the head of the shorter child standing next to her. The shorter girl is the only Black child in the photo. While this ad was supposed to champion female empowerment, it degrades the only Black person in the advertisement by posturing her like "an armrest" for the taller white child (Kim, 2016). Again, the critical questions can help children call out this racist imagery.

3. Finally, Kellogg's Corn Pops cereal printed a game on the back of the box, showing a shopping mall filled with colorful cartoon characters shaped like corn kernels. The characters are sunbathing, shopping, playing, taking photos, and skateboarding. Juxtaposed to these fun images is the only Brown-skinned character who is a janitor cleaning the floors (*Ad Age*, 2017). While explaining to children that there is nothing wrong with being a janitor, the critical questions can help children confront the negative racial message featured in this illustration.

Judge a Book by Its Cover and Words

Children are often warned not to judge a book by its cover, meaning that outward appearances are often not inner-worth indicators. However, when it comes to books (and other forms of information—including cartoons), children *should* judge them by their covers and every page. Time and again, young children's picture books and older children's textbooks contain anti-Black content. It is no wonder that too many Black children end up internalizing negative messages about Black people. Critical questions can help children critique these books.

For example, I share four of an endless number of books, including damaging anti-Black messages. Exhibit 1—*The House That George Built* (Slade, 2015)—describes how George Washington built the White House but barely mentions the significant role that African American people who were enslaved had in the building's physical construction. In Exhibits 2 and 3—*A Birthday Cake for George Washington* (Ganeshram, 2016, which was recalled by Scholastic for its unrealistic depictions) and *A Fine Dessert: Four Centuries, Four Families, One Delicious Treat* (Jenkins, 2015)—African American people who were enslaved are portrayed as smiling and seemingly happy with their situation. Exhibit 4—another example is found in a Texas state-approved high school geography book. Under a heading "Patterns of Immigration," the text describes the European slave trade as having brought "millions of *workers* from Africa to the southern United States to work on agricultural plantations" (Fernandez & Hauser, 2015, p. 10). With more than 100,000 copies of the book published, many African American children undoubtedly have been misled about the brutal history of Europeans' role in Black people's enslavement.

In each of these cases, the critical questions can help children detect what is racist and anti-Black. The more practice children have with critically questioning books, media, and other information, the more we can help them resist negative messages about Black people. They can actively learn to seek books and other texts that tell stories from Black people's perspective.

Reading the World

Currently, schools overfocus on teaching children to be passive producers and consumers of knowledge. In other words, children are told to accept whatever information is given—even when it is not accurate or contains negative stereotypes. Students are often not educated to use critical thinking to read texts to understand anti-Blackness and racism. Yet these critical thinking skills are crucial for Black children to confront racism and promote antiracism. Since this stance is not enacted by many teachers or schools, families need to empower their children to critically question the world around them.

What I Hear, I Keep

As long as racism is present, Black children need opportunities to name, question, confront, and work toward Black people's liberation. Critical questions can be used by children to talk back to anti-Black images and ideas. Families cannot always protect children from what they hear, but they can empower children to understand that not everything written or uttered needs to be kept. This is the essence of mate masie (wisdom).

References

Ad Age. (2017, October 25). *Marketer's brief: Kellogg accused of racist Corn Pops packaging.* https://adage.com/article/cmo-strategy/marketer-s-kellogg-s-accused-racist-packaging/311029

American Psychological Association. (2004, February 20). *Advertising and children.* http://www.apa.org/pubs/info/reports/advertising-children

Chan, M. (2017, October 9). Dove's "racist" ad isn't the first time the company was criticized for being offensive. *Time.* https://time.com/4974452/dove-ad-facebook-racist/

Cole, W. (2003, April–May). *Anomaly tv: Inside Bed-Stuy*. The Brooklyn Rail. https://brooklynrail.org/2003/04/local/anomaly-tv-inside-bed-stuy

Du Bois, W. E. B., & Fauset, J. (Eds.). (1920–1921). *The Brownies' book: A monthly magazine for children of the sun* [Magazine]. Du Bois & Dill.

Fernandez, M., & Hauser, C. (2015, October 5). Texas mother teaches textbook company a lesson on accuracy. *The New York Times*.

Ganeshram, R. (2016). *A birthday cake for George Washington*. Scholastic.

Jenkins, E. (2015). *A fine dessert: Four centuries, four families, one delicious treat*. Random House Children's Books.

Kim, S. (2016, April 6). *Gap pulls ad called "racist," apologizes to critics*. ABC News. https://abcnews.go.com/Business/gap-pulls-ad-called-racist-apologizes-critics/story?id=38190519

Shackelford, J. D. (1944). *My happy days*. The Associated Publishers. Inc.

Slade, S. (2015). *The house that George built*. Charlesbridge.

Tarry, E., & Ets, M. H. (1946). *My dog Rinty*. Viking Press.

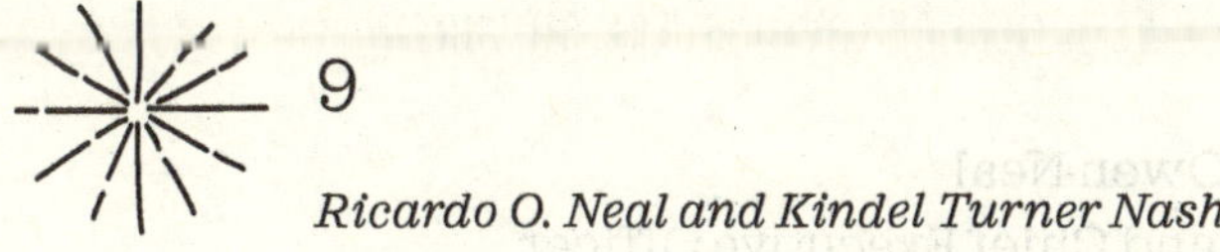

9

Ricardo O. Neal and Kindel Turner Nash

Each One, Teach One: Reflections and Lessons on Mentoring Young Men of Color

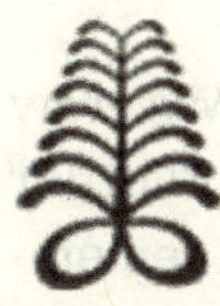

Figure 9.1. *Aya*: resourcefulness and endurance
Source: http://www.adinkra.org/htmls/adinkra/aya.htm

To My Boys, I haven't yet entirely told you my story and why I've dedicated my life to serving you. This chapter is a letter to you. I write it because I want to share the story of how I came to the work of mentoring and supporting young men, and why I think your success is an essential ingredient to building vibrant communities. For you and all those that read this, I hope you see how *each one can teach one*. Aya is the West African Adinkra symbol representing the fern (see Figure 9.1). Ferns are hardy plants that can grow in difficult places. There are lessons to be shared, and I hope you can use them as you grow and consider how you might best serve others. It has been my honor to serve you, and I commend you for your strength in the face of adversity.

Ricardo Owen Neal
Founder and Chief Executive Officer
We Will All Rise, Inc.

Early Years: Jamaica

Boys,[1] the 11-year-old boy who came to the United States so many summers ago is ever-present in who I am, what I do, and how I do what I do. Living in Jamaica was idyllic and sad at the same time. I lived with both my parents and my seven siblings. We had a wonderful house with indoor plumbing, a washroom, and a veranda that wrapped around the house's front. I would say there was a back veranda, but my older siblings would likely tell me that my memory is off. The details have become foggy over the decades.

In Jamaica, we raised pigs, chickens, and goats. We grew sugarcane, almonds, cherries, coconuts, mangos, and other fruits and vegetables that have escaped my memory. I remember the wash lady coming to help my mother and the guy who would cut the grass with a machete. We were happy in Jamaica. Our seven national heroes were Black women and men, and they were fierce. They built a vibrant culture, and we reveled in our beauty and success. Teachers, doctors, bankers, politicians, lunch ladies, taxi drivers, and entertainers were all Black, brilliant, beautiful, and proud.

Yet, for all that Jamaica had to offer, my parents knew they had to leave. Education ends in eighth grade if students fail to pass the high school common entrance exam. Jamaica was a violent place in the 1980s because of deep-rooted conflicts between the People's National Party and the Jamaican Labour Party. I remember the rat-a-tat-tat of machine guns at night, gunmen running through our property, all of us huddled

---

1   The use of the word *boy* should not be mistaken as a sign of disrespect. When I use the word, there is a history of mutual respect and admiration that the young men will understand.

together in my parents' room. When it was not the real risk of gun slaughter, it was an entire community running, chests heaving from the suffocating smell of sulfuric acid blanketing the community. We had to leave our home despite its beauty and affirming images of brilliance and success.

Middle Years: Finding a New Home and Discovering Hate

We arrived in Lawrence, Massachusetts, during the mid-1980s. Historic mills, massive, sturdy, and repurposed, dominated the city. What struck me about Lawrence were the flags lining Essex Street. In my mind, the flags represented respect for diverse cultures. They meant that all were welcomed regardless of national origin. The flags suggested that there was a home for everyone in Lawrence. Yet I realized something else—for the first time in my life—everyone was not Black. I felt alone and outside for the first time ever, but I was okay because I went home to a strong family every day.

I started cleaning up city parks and rivers and got involved in student government. I cared about my new home. I wanted to do my part to improve Lawrence. Still, I quickly learned that not everyone in my community actually wanted me or my help. I can still remember an older white lady telling me to "go back to where you are from" after a school committee meeting. There was also a time when I was walking home, and a bunch of white boys said something about "the nigger." That was my first time hearing the word. I knew it was a terrible thing, yet I didn't overthink about those boys. The foundation for loving and taking care of my community was firmly established. I already knew I had a voice, and I had every intention of using it.

I enrolled in the University of Massachusetts at Amherst, and the nigger thing followed me to campus. How should a young man react to find the word nigger and human feces smeared on his dorm room door? Frankly, I felt protected by the Black community and other students of color who felt rage and wanted to be left alone just to live. I refused to let hate and ignorance consume me. There was too much to be done. By the time I left college, I was secure in my identity as a leader and an advocate. More important, I'd accomplished more than my parents ever imagined possible.

In the Now: The Power of Love and Community

Gentlemen, as I reflect on lessons learned from my two decades of mentoring work, I now realize that I have spent most of my time in communities fighting hate. The closer my community work took me to street outreach—visiting jails, talking to young men about their lives—the more I realized that our Black boys and other people of color seemed to be dying at an alarming rate. In fact, one out of every 1,000 young Black men is the fatal victim of police violence. At the same time, other young men and women of color are also more likely to die at the police's hands (Edwards et al., 2019). As I visited juvenile detention centers and prisons, the stark reality was that Black men were the primary occupants. At the same time, the community was fighting to save their lives. I had no choice but to join the fight. I sat on various boards and part-nered with law enforcement. I encouraged folks in my circle to get involved. Over time, I settled on education as the most meaningful way to impact change. My combined experiences led me to found We Will All Rise (All Rise), an organization focused on mentoring young men of color and dedicated to educating, elevating, and empowering our community mem-bers to surmount social, economic, and institutional barriers.

Advice to Young Men Rising

Boys, I wanted to share my story because as you chart your course in life, I want you to recognize that, like aya, the fern, we can grow and emerge stronger from difficult circumstances.

We go about our fight for justice in different ways, but we must be unified in our efforts at the end of the day, always showing respect for our brothers. Joyce King (2005) highlighted the principle that "we exist as African People, an ethnic family. Our perspective must be centered in that reality" (p. 20). With this knowledge of the importance of viewing ourselves as a family whose collective survival is more important than individual survival, I offer these words of advice to you as you consider ways to join together in the fight and carry forward the mentoring work:

- You will have justified anger, and some of you will take to the streets to push back hard against hate. I salute you in your fight.

- Some of you will use the written word to fight back against disinformation and misrepresentation. Well-meaning white allies will want to change your words to fit their narrative. Resist that approach at all times because they do not know your struggle, and they often perpetuate negative stereotypes.

- Those who take to the pulpit—your words and actions are divine, not because of you but because you have been chosen as a vessel to deliver God's words. You are our spiritual warriors because we need unconditional love and protection.

- Gentlemen, elevate and champion those waging the fight inside corporate America, where brothers are often fighting the good fight in isolation, misunderstood by professional peers, and considered a "sellout" by many.

- We are one community on many different paths to right the wrongs that have been wrought upon us. Love and respect for each other. Do not tear each other down in the fight.

Ubuntu: Mentoring Men of Color

Nobel Peace Prize–winner Desmond Tutu (1999) remarked, "When we want to give high praise to someone, we say, 'Yu u nobuntu' [So-and-so has ubuntu]" (p. 31). Ubuntu is a South African principle that means "humanness." Exhibiting ubuntu is carried out by prioritizing relationships with others, so it is associated with the phrase "I am because we are" (Metz, 2011). When thinking about mentoring Black and other young men of color, I have learned the most important lesson is to prioritize relationships with the boys as the center of the work. That is why most of this chapter is a letter to the boys. In this section, building foremost on ubuntu's principle, we lay out foundational ideas that have been important, hoping others can build on it in doing mentoring work:

- **Build an ecosystem.** Consider how you might engage barbershops, convenience stores, religious institutions, schools, gyms, or other businesses.

- **Engage women.** In our experience, Black men will not succeed unless Black women succeed. Black women will lead in critical ways that demand respect and support.

- **Create rituals and celebrations.** It is essential to believe in the brilliance of young Black men. Let them know that they will face setbacks in life, yet significant things await. Publicly celebrate them to showcase their gifts. Create annual events like dinners and tie-tying ceremonies to celebrate mentoring activities. Share written pieces that honor Black men and encourage them to create original works. Without exception, always honor those who walked the path with you when mentoring young Black men.

- **Be accessible to younger brothers.** Those who are younger than you will admire you and want to emulate what you have accomplished. Respond with love and appreciation when a young man wants to be in your presence. Listen carefully when a more youthful brother approaches you. He may not have all the right words, but he wants to learn. Help him understand the value of being healthy and productive, for he wants to become a responsible man.

- **Explore and experiment with the unfamiliar.** Engage mentees through going to plays, athletic events, and participating in service events together. Travel to new places (domestically and internationally) whenever you have a chance. Interacting with different cultures and communities will strengthen minds and souls and increase the commitment to creating a better world.

- **Hold each other accountable.** Get to know the brothers you support. Set expectations based on their life circumstances and call them out when they fail to meet those expectations. When you know that they can process your feedback, help young brothers to self-correct. Point them to resources when you do not have the answers. Do not tear down your brothers.

- **Stay the course.** You will become angry when young brothers do not heed your advice. They will make life-altering mistakes and disappointment will set in. It is in the most challenging moments where you double down (pull back when necessary but do not abandon) and let them know that you love them and stand ready to support them when they are right.

I (Ricardo) encourage those of you who do mentoring work to find your brothers' and sisters' band as you assume greater responsibilities in your life. They will stand with you when you confront difficult times. For almost a decade now, four Black men, Ivan Douglas, Mark Nash, LaVaughn Turner, and Maurice Wilkins, have been my partners in this beautiful struggle and, most recently, Calvin Lewis. I honor each man because they have been tireless in their work with a fierce commitment to young men of color. Finally, while the reality of a brilliant and vibrant Black culture in Jamaica is seared in my memory, I have faced anti-Black hate and oppression in this country. Yet I am like the fern, aya, growing in a difficult place, and I fight because I have been offered many opportunities in America. I refuse to quit because my community inspires me. I see that I am because we are, and I am relentless about pursuing the promise of us.

References

Edwards, F., Lee, H., & Esposito, M. (2019). Risk of being killed by police use of force in the United States by age, race–ethnicity, and sex. *Proceedings of the National Academy of Sciences, 116*(34), 16793–16798.

King, J. E. (Ed.). (2005). *Black education: A transformative research and action agenda for the new century*. Routledge.

Metz, T. (2011). Ubuntu as a moral theory and human rights in South Africa. *African Human Rights Law Journal, 11*(2), 532–559.

Tutu, D. (1999). *No future without forgiveness*. Random House.

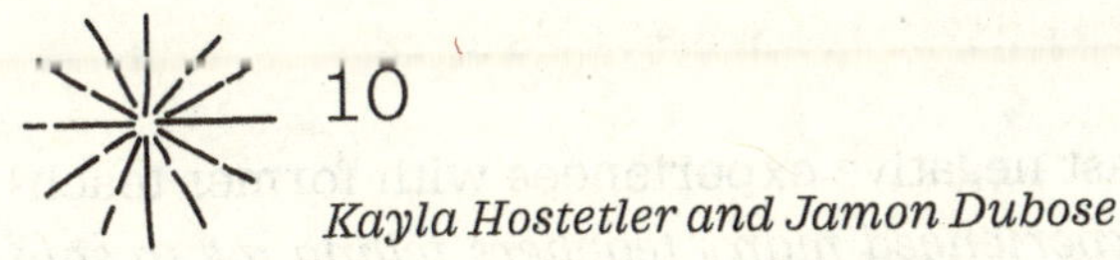
10

Kayla Hostetler and Jamon Dubose

We Be Family

It was the end of the school year, and I, Kayla, adjusted Mello's tie for graduation. I had tears in my eyes, trying desperately to hold back my emotions. Mello looked at me and said, "What's wrong, Ma?" I just shook my head and replied, "Nothing." He responded, "I know something is bothering you. What's up?" Sighing, I said, "I am proud of you, but this is a hard day for me. You'll leave here and I won't see you again. I'm just a teacher." He responded, "Nah, we be family." As much as I learned over the 4 years from Mello and his classmates, I missed a critical cultural understanding. I quickly responded, "But, I'm not your real mama. When you come home from college, you will stop and see your real family." Mello just smiled and shook his head. He looked at me and slowly said, "We are family. We were family. We will always be family." Mello is now 24 years old, and he was right. We *be* family. He and his classmates are still my family. We still spend time together, have gatherings, and text often. Teaching students like Mello has been one of the biggest blessings of my life.

Community Building

Black students often experience curricular and instructional violence in schools. As a white female teacher, many Black students and parents enter my room guarded and carrying the trauma of past negative experiences with former teachers. *I, Jamon, experienced many teachers telling me to shut up, be quiet, and stop talking out of turn. I would often be reprimanded for trying to work with my peers. They would tell me I was too loud. I was sent to sit in the hall or kicked out of the classroom, missing the instruction completely. This made me defensive when I would meet new teachers because I had to figure out how they would treat me.* Building a community where students feel comfortable, loved, respected, and trust each other is my (Kayla's) number one goal.

Décor

Working to build a community begins with focusing on the physical meeting space of the community. I, Kayla, work to make sure that my classroom's physical environment reflects the students I teach and that it has supplies they need to be successful. I make sure to purchase and supply students with novels with main characters that reflect their race and gender readily available in my classroom library. I display these books that show characters that look like them across the room. There are pictures of former students shaped in hearts on the walls. The desks are always set up in three to four groups, so students can work together on all tasks. Every supply that a student could possibly need is at their disposal to use for the entire year. There is a prayer wall dedicated to Tupac—my favorite rapper and poet. There are Adinkra symbols across the top of the whiteboard. After students complete their affirmation flags the first week, their affirmations are posted in the room for the entire year as a reminder to themselves. Our room also has lotion for the students to use at any time and good brands of tissues. There is a snack closet for any student who needs a little nourishment to get through the class. A charging station is set up for their cell phones if they need to charge before they leave for after-school activities or work. I intentionally purchase items for my classroom that will make my students comfortable. I want to show them that I care about their needs as a person, not just the content.

I, Jamon, when first walking into Ms. H's room, was surprised. I never saw a teacher who had a room that looked like hers. My first thoughts were she's different and she must have a thing for Tupac. I saw books that had Black teens on the cover. I noticed that the desks were in groups and all my other teachers had rows. The classroom felt like home. My other classrooms felt like a typical school with the occasional educational posters that said, "If you can dream it, you can do it" or "Deadlines are closer than they appear." I could tell she put some time into her room. Then I found out she had snacks, drinks, and school supplies we could have. She even bought us each our own notebook and folder. I had heard from older students that she was different, but it was another experience to walk into the classroom and see it.

Taking time to make the classroom warm and welcoming for Black students is just one small step to building a community. Classrooms, just like other community spaces, can be set up to show a commitment to social connectedness and to demonstrate love for the whole child or person. See the Guidelines for Community (Table 10.1).

Table 10.1. Guidelines for Community

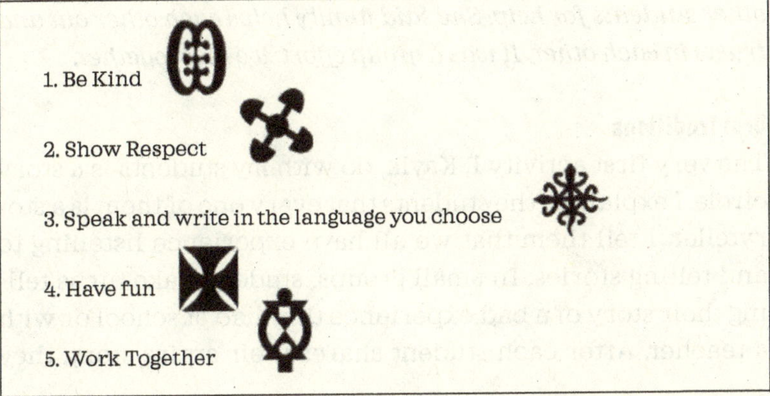

The first day of classes at school is boring. Every year is the same routine sitting at a desk and hearing the rules each teacher created. Don't do this, don't do that, if you don't do your work you get a zero. No late work. Ms. H did not do that. She simply put up her guidelines for the community. She said that she did not have a syllabus. Her expectations were as difficult and as simple as the five guidelines she posted. This was a bit shocking to me, Jamon. She moved directly into a story circle.

The guideline that really meant a lot to me was "Speak and write in the language you choose." Ms. H taught us the beauty of using our home languages. She even did some lessons on African American Vernacular. She taught all the kids the rules of the language. I didn't even know the way I talked was considered an official language. I didn't realize it had rules. Ms. H was the only English teacher who never corrected the way I spoke. She never said it was wrong. She let us be us. She showed us how to use Standard English but always gave us a choice in which language we used to turn in assignments. I still wonder how she graded assignments written in Spanish.

Another class guideline that spoke to me was "Work together." We were always permitted to lean on each other for support and help. Ms. H never told us we could not help each other. This was very different from my previous experiences, where I was told to stop talking to my peers. She would often redirect a student to other students for help. She said family helps each other out and trusts in each other. It was a group effort; we rose together.

Oral Traditions

The very first activity I, Kayla, do with my students is a story circle. I explain to the students that every one of them is a storyteller. I tell them that we all have experience listening to and telling stories. In small groups, students take turns telling their story of a bad experience they had at school or with a teacher. After each student shares their entire story, they make a chart of what they had in common. I then ask them to share a story of the good experience they had in school or with a teacher. Again, after each student shares, they make a common list. Then as a class, each group selects a speaker to share the highlights of the stories they heard. We keep a running list of the bad and the good on the whiteboard. Together, as a class community, we create a list of norms and experiences that we want to have for the school year. Throughout the year, I use story circles in different ways. Another example is after reading *All American Boys* (Reynolds & Kiely, 2016), I ask the students to tell a story about an interaction they had with a police officer. Story circles draw on oral traditions and give Black students a space to share their experiences, histories, and truths.

Story circles remind me, Jamon, of talking with my family. They allow everyone to listen and learn from each other. We often laughed a lot when we are doing story circles. They helped us bond, get to know each other, and get comfortable. They also had the power to tell some hard truths. They bring weight to the room sometimes. I remember doing a story circle after reading The Hate U Give *(Thomas, 2017). I was in a group with another Black boy and two white girls. The one white girl's dad was a cop. She told a story about her dad helping a local homeless man. Then it was the other Black boy's turn. He told the story of riding his bike and a cop made him stop. The cop searched him along the road, basically pulled down his pants, and told him he matched a description. His story brought weight to the room. They both spoke their truths, and they were able to gain some new truths from their differences.*

Identity Poetry

Following the story circles, I, Kayla, intentionally plan to build a community with my students through identity poetry and identity assignments. One of the first identity poems that students work on is a "Where I Am From" poem. This poem tells a story about each student's home and some important aspects of their identity. Students share their poems in small groups and have an opportunity to share their poems with the larger group. I, Kayla, always make sure to share my own piece with the students. To show them, I am willing to be vulnerable and share my experiences as well. We create name poems, in which students share the meaning and stories of their names. They write traditional African praise poems, in which students honor an important person in their lives for their skills and/or personality. They write "Raised by Women" poems, in which they honor the people that raised them. They create rings of identity to show the visual rings they bring with them into spaces and deconstruct how they shape their responses. They create affirmations and make a pennant with their affirmations that are displayed all year within the classroom. They share in their small groups and as a large group, taking risks sharing who they are.

The poetry that we created at the beginning of the year and all throughout the year was powerful. It let me, Jamon, tell my story. It helped me show my classmates that there is more to me than what people think. I remember one girl who went to school with me for years and said to me after a week of poetry sharing that she didn't know that I had some challenging experiences. She thought I was just always the happy-go-lucky class clown. It also taught me about my other classmates and showed me I, too, was wrong about some of my perceptions about them. The sharing helped me break down some prejudices I had too.

Text Selections and History

After building a strong community, I, Kayla, intentionally select books that reflect my classroom students. I make sure to include contemporary books and novels such as the following:

- *A Long Way Gone* by Ishmael Beah (2008)

- *The Hate U Give* by Angie Thomas (2017)

- *Dear Martin* by Nic Stone (2017)

- *Things Fall Apart* by Chinua Achebe (1958)

- *Purple Hibiscus* by Chimamanda Adichie (2003)

- *A Rose That Grew from Concrete* by Tupac (1999)

I select these contemporary novels and provide Black students space and time to read about their people's beauty and strength.

The only time I, Jamon, read novels with Black main characters was in Ms. Hostetler's class and in a few elementary classes. In middle school, I did not read one novel that had a Black main character, and in high school, all the other teachers taught boring books about mostly White men. I only learned Black history in school, focusing on two eras, slavery and civil rights history. I never learned Black history pre-enslavement or after the civil rights era or even between the two eras. Ms. H's class was the first time I heard of an Adinkra symbol. I didn't know anything about ancient Africa. I had to teach myself about these topics. I still don't really know how to process my feelings related to this gap in my education. It is hard to understand how so much of Black people's history is left out of textbooks and not taught in history class. As many times as I have learned about slavery and the civil rights era, there was time to learn about ancient Africa.

Speak Up/Stand Up

Through the focus of creating a community, in my, Kayla's, classroom and using African Diaspora as the focus of the class's literature, I give students the space to share their truths and begin standing up against inequities. They create their own literature pieces to share their stories that are often silenced. Their final project for my class is a research project on a social issue they see within their community. They work in groups to conduct a literature review, collect their own data, and develop a plan to act. They also are required to take some sort of action. Through this project, students engage in verve (lively action) and communalism (committing to others).

My, Jamon's, action project changed me. I became empowered and confident in sharing my truth and helping my community. It showed me the power and strength of my community and engaging in community building with others. It helped me understand ubuntu, I am because we are. I started a mentor program in my neighborhood for young Black males, and now I am the youth director of a local youth activist group that I helped form. Ms. H's room became a second home where I grew up.

Mello, Jamon, Nikole, and all my Black students taught me, Kayla, that there is strength and power in unity. Together, we formed a bond that transcended the classroom walls. We built a community and a family. A family that still gathers and helps each other. We practiced and lived and continue to practice an important aspect of African Diaspora and culture: communalism. We were, are, and will always be family (see Figures 10.1–10.4).

Figure 10.1. *Nkonsonkonson*: symbol of unity and human relations, a reminder to contribute to the community and that in unity lies strength. *Source:* http://www.adinkra.org/htmls/adinkra/nkon.htm

Figure 10.2. Jamon and Mrs. Hostetler

Figure 10.3. Jamon and Mrs. Hostetler

Figure 10.4. Jamon walking Mrs. Hostetler's daughter to her first basketball game

References

Achebe, C. (1958). *Things fall apart*. William Heinemann Ltd.

Adichie, C. (2003). *Purple hibiscus*. Algonquin Books Kachifo Limited.

Beah, I. (2008). *A long way gone: Memoirs of a boy soldier*. Sarah Crichton.

Reynolds, J., & Kiely, B. (2016). *All American boys*. Atheneum.

Shakur, T. (1999). *The rose that grew from concrete*. MTV books.

Stone, N. (2017). *Dear Martin*. Random House Children's Books.

Thomas, A. (2017). *The hate you give*. Balzer & Bray.

Shayla Calhoun and Joy Howard

The Crown on Your Head: Teaching African Diaspora Literacy Through Hair

Being Natural is not a statement. It is the closest I can get to being myself.

—Curlyhairlounge.com

Remove the kinks from your mind, not your hair.

—Marcus Garvey

The chapter-opening statements speak to the necessity for hair freedom among Black youth—freedom from judgment, ridicule, and punishment because of hair choices. For far too many Black children in schools, hair has been a site of racialized violence. In response to this reality, we asked ourselves *how teachers (including first teachers [families] and community teachers) rewrite a narrative that affirms natural hair?* Pulling from Gloria Boutte's and her coauthors' (2017) work on African Diaspora Literacies based on A. Wade Boykin's (1983) research on the principles that follow, we put forward three dimensions of African culture as an entry point into this discussion:

- Expressive individualism

- Affect

- Harmony

This chapter highlights examples of conflict over Black hair in recent news, scholarship on the topic, and propositions for creating an inviting space for adults and children to learn about, discuss, and welcome Black hairstyles into various learning spaces.

The Right to Our Hair in Schools: A Brief Overview

Devastating disparities in school discipline have been noted and discussed all over the country (Alexander, 2012; Blad & Harwin, 2017). Too often, Black students are punished for "violating" subjective school dress code policies, specifically related to hairstyles. Black students have been scrutinized for their head coverings and hairstyles, signifying natural and cultural norms:

- High school senior, Lawrence Charles, was suspended for wearing his du-rag to school (*The Grio*, 2018).

- Wrestler Andrew Johnson was forced to cut off his dreadlocks during a wrestling match (Blackistone, 2018).

- Six-year-old Clinton Stanley Jr. was sent home from his first day of school because of his dreadlocks (Morgan-Smith, 2018).

- Thirteen-year-old J. T's teacher colored his hair with a black marker (Sparks, 2019), and 8-year-old Marian Scott was excluded from school pictures because of her new red hair extensions (Alsharif, 2019).

- Pictures featuring Black hairstyles at Narvie J. Harris Elementary School in Decatur, Georgia, demonstrated what *not* to wear to school (Vigdor, 2019).

Attacks on Black children's bodies, minds, and spirits occur every day. Black students' hair is not a problem to be fixed or managed. Colonizing and oppressive messages embedded in Eurocratic practices and policies must be changed (King & Swartz, 2015). Punishing Black students for their hairstyles and head covering choices is both demeaning and exclusionary. These practices and policies violate children's rights to an education, and change is necessary.

Connecting to a Broader Conversation

Hair has always been an integral part of African American culture and identity, with deep African roots that existed before slavery (Brooks & McNair, 2015; Byrd & Tharps, 2001). Hair care and styles are an important part of bonding and building relationships with the community. Discussions about hair in the school curriculum are essential to all students' well-being, especially Black students. A promising move toward justice is the CROWN Act (Creating a Respectful and Open Workplace for Natural Hair), which began in January 2020, to eliminate institutional biases based on discrimination against natural hair (Blaes & Domek, 2019).

The Call for Teachers and Youth Workers to Do Better

Educators must reflect on Black hair as a cultural expression site, a human right, and a strength. Educators must work toward practices that invite students to be fully engaged as a part of the learning community. This includes their hair. Children's experiences with their hair, whether positive or negative, will influence how they see themselves and the world around them. Black children need to be exposed to literary works that feature characters that look like them because it shapes how they view the world and themselves. Understanding the significance of hair in literary works is essential because of hair matters (Brooks & McNair, 2015; Edwards, 2005).

To confront the damaging messages in society, as a whole, and school spaces, specifically, we must build on Black culture's strengths as we teach and learn. The Adinkra symbol *duafe*—the wooden comb, which symbolizes beauty and cleanliness or looking one's best (see Figure 11.1)—is a value expressed in West African culture. We take up this symbol to indicate the cultural emphasis on hairstyles as integral for defining beauty from an Afrocentric perspective. Building on this concept, we focus on several African principles to inform curriculum and teaching relative to Black hair in learning spaces: expressive individualism, affect, and harmony.

Figure 11.1. Duafe—"wooden comb"—a symbol of beauty and cleanliness representing looking one's best
Source: http://www.adinkra.org/htmls/adinkra/duafe.htm

Boutte and coauthors (2017) explain *expressive individualism* as the cultivation of a distinctive personality and proclivity for spontaneous and genuine personal expression. *Affect* emphasizes emotions and feelings and sensitivity to emotional cues and the tendency to be emotionally expressive. *Harmony* refers to the notion that one's fare is interrelated with other elements in the scheme of things so that humankind and nature are harmonically conjoined. We apply these African principles to real-life examples of how each of these dimensions has come to life in Shayla's classroom.

Our Connections With Black Hair

Shayla

I am an African American elementary school teacher, graduate student, and parent of four children. I have taught for more than 10 years in kindergarten through third grade and worked extensively with many fourth- and fifth-grade students through after-school extracurricular activities such as basketball and our school's step team. As I am a parent with four children, hair is very much a part of my life. My exploration of Black hair in the classroom began in 2018. I made two major life changes. I made the decision to go natural and to start a doctoral program in educational leadership. This was a pivotal moment in my personal and professional journey. In my returning natural journey, I realized that returning my hair to its natural state was much deeper than I had ever perceived. It caused me to evaluate who I am and what defines me as an individual, which led me to where I am now exploring natural hair in an educational setting.

Joy

My exploration of Black hair in the classroom has grown out of three sources of inspiration. As a white mother scholar (Howard et al., in press), my scholarly interests are intimately connected to my role as the mother of three Black mixed-race sons. I have observed and mediated some of their experiences inside and outside of schools where hair has been a primary entry point for how people see my children racially (e.g., strangers stating, "Wow, his hair is curly. Can I touch it? What is he?") and how they express themselves racially (e.g., one of my sons decided to get cornrows before entering a new school to assert his African ancestry). My ongoing work about Black mixed-race children's experiences in schools (Howard, 2022) affirmed hair as a primary symbol that teachers, students, and the school community use to ascribe race to Black mixed-race students. Shayla's inquiry about Black hair was fascinating to me as a mother, learner, instructor, and advisor. We describe how Shayla has applied three key principles: expressive individualism, affect, and harmony by intentionally affirming Black hair in the classroom.

African Principles in the Curriculum

Expressive Individualism

As a facilitator, I encourage students to see themselves not just as individuals but as amazing individuals. When I did the "big chop," I had to reimagine my hair. I had to figure out what to do with it. I had to get accustomed to wearing and creating new hairstyles such as pineapples, buns, and free curls. I noticed that my students and other teachers saw me differently. Some students seemed to admire my hair while others appeared confused and expressed their confusion. I began to question my beauty and uniqueness, but about 9 months into the transition, I decided that I would love my natural hair.

Expressive individualism, the cultivation of a distinctive personality and genuine personal expression is demonstrated in the book *I Love My Hair* by Natasha Anastasia Tarpley (2003). The book tells a story about the importance of loving your hair because it is your hair. I ask children to create portraits of themselves and use descriptive adjectives (e.g., curly) to complete a writing assignment. In a classroom setting or community space, expressive individualism begins when students are free to show who they are as individuals. Making connections to art and history, having open discussions about the process of braiding or experiences at barbershops, or featuring literature that displays unique styles would all support a celebration of expressive individualism.

Improvisation

Improvisation includes the substitution of alternatives that are more sensitive to Black culture. Exposing students to various narratives allows them to see elements of themselves through the characters and people they read about. Most students know about or have read some version of "Goldilocks and the Three Bears," but Yolanda King's (2015), *Curlilocks and the Big Bad Hairbrush* is a version told through the lens of a curly-haired Brown-skinned girl. Books that reflect the students I teach increase students' confidence. Stories like this one can teach a variety of skills and concepts such as central message, comparing and contrasting, creative writing, or as part of a book study exploring different versions of "Goldilocks and the Three Bears." Students can work in small groups using props and other materials to retell the story while identifying the characters, setting, and other important key details or to use a reader's theater format. One year, my students wrote their own version and performed it for their families at school—creating their own background props and making a dessert. Students and teachers at the school were also invited to attend. Reflecting on this event made me realize the importance of improvisation and the necessity to be more attuned to Black culture. Allowing Black students to star as themselves with their natural hairstyles can greatly impact their self-esteem.

Affect

Affect emphasizes emotions and feelings and sensitivity to emotional cues as well as the tendency to be emotionally expressive. As a Black educator, who has natural hair, I have become highly sensitive to my students' feelings and emotional cues. I have noticed students who have tried to hide or avoid classmates because they have been ashamed of their hair, such as students hiding in the bathroom or repeatedly going to the bathroom to style their hair or trying to cover up their natural locks.

The struggle to get your hair just right can be paralyzing. These experiences made me realize that appearance is very important to children, including how their hair looks. I have begun to reflect on my memories as a child, and my own current hair experiences, and as a mother of two girls and two boys with natural hair. I have realized that my experiences were not just my own. This gives me a sense of pride in who I am as an educator and the diverse skill set I bring to the table. Books that support affect include *I Am Enough!* by Grace Byers (2018), and *I Like Myself!* by Karen Beaumont (2010). Students can reflect on themes of self-esteem, empathy, respect, and celebrating uniqueness in reading responses. I have had students write and share what makes them unique. Prompting students with sentence starters, such as *If I could describe myself using three words . . . , I am unique because . . . ,* and *I like myself because . . . ,* can help them conceptualize their thoughts. Educators must be aware of the effects—of the emotions, feelings, and needs of Black students.

Harmony

Students should be actively engaged in and considered while planning instructional content. The inclusion of children of all races with a common goal in mind (harmony) is essential. Texts must be carefully selected and activities must be intentional. If students can't envision themselves or relate to a literature piece, then harmony is not achieved. Harmony in a classroom setting could include students using the following books to write their own unique stories, write or draw what harmony looks like in their own communities, and explain responsibilities as a group or community member:

- *One Love* (Marley, 2014)

- *Hair Love* (Cherry, 2019)

- *Don't Touch My Hair* (Miller, 2019). Students can discuss the importance of respecting others' possessions, including hair.

Conclusion

We hope that readers can envision themselves as catalysts to change the narrative about Black hair by acknowledging that this narrative includes everyone—Black and non-Black natural hair. We encourage readers to adapt these examples to unique teaching and learning contexts and expand on these dimensions to affirm Black children's strength and beauty, including their hair, in our community, educational, and home spaces.

References

Alexander, M. (2012). *The new Jim Crow: Mass incarceration in the age of color-blindness*. The New Press.

Alsharif, M. (2019, November 20). *Michigan 8-year-old gets photo shoot after being denied school picture for her hair extensions*. CNN. https://www.cnn.com/2019/11/19/us/michigan-8-year-old-photo-shoot-trnd/index.html

Beaumont, K. (2010). *I like myself!* HMH Books for Young Readers.

Blackistone, K. B. (2018, December 28). Wrestler being forced to cut dreadlocks was manifestation of decades of racial desensitization. *Washington Post*. https://www.washingtonpost.com/sports/wrestler-being-forced-to-cut-dreadlocks-was-manifestation-of-decades-of-racial-desensitization/2018/12/27/66f520ba-0a10-11e9-85b6-41c0fe0c5b8f_story.html?noredirect=on&utm_term=.a1eb2bc98c06

Blad, E., & Harwin, A. (2017). Black students more likely to be arrested at school. Policing America's schools. *Education Week, 36*(19), 1–12.

Blaes, L. J., & Domek, N. L. (2019, August 22). *A heads up on the CROWN Act: Employees' natural hairstyles now protected*. The National Law Review. https://www.natlawreview.com/article/heads-crown-act-employees-natural-hairstyles-now-protected

Boutte, G. S., Johnson, G. L., Wynter-Hoyt, K., & Uyoata, U. E. (2017). Using African Diaspora Literacy to heal and restore the souls of Black folks. *International Critical Childhood Policy Studies Journal, 6*(1), 66–79.

Boykin, A. W. (1983). The academic performance of Afro-American children. In J. Spence (Ed.), *Achievement and achievement motives* (pp. 323–371). Freeman.

Brooks, W. M., & McNair, J. C. (2015). "Combing" through representations of black girls' hair in African American children's literature. *Gender and Education, 46*(3), 296–307. http://doi10.1080/09540253.2016.12 21888

Byers, G. (2018). *I am enough*. Balzer & Bray Publishing.

Byrd, A., & Tharps, L. (2001). *Hair story: Untangling the roots of Black hair in America*. St. Martin's Press.

Calhoun, S. (2020). *The crown on your head: Teaching African diaspora literacy through hair* [Unpublished manuscript]. University of Southern Indiana.

Cherry, M. A. (2019). *Hair love*. Kokila.

Edwards, D. (2005, Spring). "Doing hair" and literacy in an afterschool reading and writing workshop for African American adolescent girls. *Afterschool Matters*, (4), 42–50.

The Grio. (2018, April 20). *Arizona high schooler suspended for wearing durag says his punishment is racist*. https://thegrio.com/2018/04/20/arizona-principal-suspends-student-durag/

Howard, J. (2022). Just playin': Black mixed-race boys and the injustices of boyhood. *Race Ethnicity and Education, 25*(5), 703–721. https://doi.org/10.1080/13613324.2019.1679760

Howard, J., Thompson, C., & Nash, K. (In press). Mother (space) scholar (space): Poetic inquiries of motherscholaring. *Qualitative Studies in Education*.

King, J. E., & Swartz, E. E. (2015). *The Afrocentric praxis of teaching for freedom: Connecting culture to learning*. Routledge.

King, Y. (2015). *Curlilocks and the big bad hairbrush*. Tangled Press.

Marley, C. (2014). *One love*. Chronicle Books.

Miller, S. (2019). *Don't touch my hair*. Little, Brown Books for Readers.

Morgan-Smith, K. (2018, August 16). *Adorable six-year-old boy banned from school for dreadlocks*. The Grio. https://thegrio.com/2018/08/16/adorable-six-year-old-black-boy-banned-from-school-for-dread-locks/

Sparks, H. (2019, August 20). School forced Black student to "Sharpie in" his haircut: Lawsuit. *New York Post*. https://nypost.com/2019/08/20/school-forced-black-student-to-sharpie-in-his-haircut-lawsuit/

Tarpley, N. A. (2003). *I love my hair*. LB Kids.

Vigdor, N. (2019, August 3). Georgia elementary school is accused of racial insensitivity over hairstyle guidelines display. *New York Times*. https://www.nytimes.com/2019/08/03/us/hairstyles-black-students-appropriate-inappropriate.html

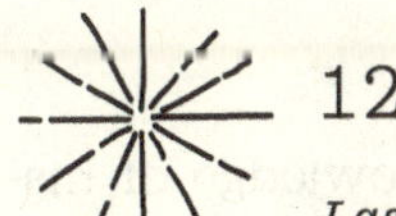

Lasana D. Kazembe, Leslie K. Etienne,
and Tambra O. Jackson

Teaching Our Children About Blackness in the World

In 2006, *National Geographic* issued a famous survey to measure geographic literacy rates among young adults worldwide. Sadly, the lack of global knowledge (e.g., recognizing names and locations of countries, continents, bodies of water) remains a serious problem—especially among U.S. students. Geographic literacy (referred to as *geoliteracy*) describes the multiple ways in which people understand, interpret, and interact with the world. When students possess geoliteracy skills, they can also better assess themselves and their place in the world. When geoliteracy is incorporated into education, students (especially younger children) benefit by gaining a deeper understanding of

- world cultures and historically significant events,

- diverse ways of learning and interacting with content, and

- interconnections across multiple diverse areas of culture (e.g., arts, cuisine, language).

For Black children, geoliteracy is especially important because of its potential to expand and deepen (particularly within community learning spaces) their knowledge of history and culture. Liberatory Black community learning spaces in the United States (e.g., African Free Schools, Citizenship Schools, Freedom Schools, Sabbath Schools, Midnight Schools) have played an important role and have a proud legacy of learning and resilience outside of formal school. In this chapter, we describe two educational programs: Freedom Schools and elev8te. Specifically, we discuss how each is focused on the African Diaspora and enacted within extra-curricular contexts.

Figure 12.1. *Nea onnim no sua a ohu*—"one who does not know can know from learning" (knowledge, lifelong education, and continued quest for knowledge)
Source: http://www.adinkra.org/htmls/adinkra/neao.htm

The African Diaspora refers to people of African origin who live outside of the African continent and who are spread throughout the world. Here are a few population estimates of people of African ancestry in the Diaspora:

- North America: 39 million

- Latin America: 113 million

- Caribbean: 14 million

- Europe: 3.5 million

Those big numbers include large groups of Africans located throughout French Guiana, Colombia, Dominica, as well as Lisbon. Now, if those faraway places seem totally unfamiliar to you, then you are not alone. One of the basic goals of geoliteracy, to make the unfamiliar familiar, affirms the cultural principle of the nea onnim no sua a ohu, the Adinkra symbol shown in Figure 12.1, to engage in a continued quest for knowledge.

When it comes to educating Black youth, we must locate and develop creative ways to keep them engaged. Black youth must understand the world around them and how people and ideas are interconnected. Geoliteracy is crucial because it enhances Black youth's preparedness to acquire a deeper understanding of cultures and enhanced reasoning skills within and across learning contexts. It provides a gateway for positive Black student learning breakthroughs.

Collectively, Freedom Schools and elev8te represent powerful models for deepening and enriching Black children and youth's education. For example, there is value for African American students to be engaged in deep learning about the living legacy of Ella Baker and the history and impact of the Tuskegee model. Similarly, there is value in African American students learning about how Haitian artists created a literary and artistic movement that challenged racism and global imperialism. As we reveal, there are lots of rich, fascinating connections and interconnections within and across both contexts.

Figure 12.2. *mate masie*—"What I hear, I keep" (wisdom, knowledge, prudence)
Source: http://www.adinkra.org/htmls/adinkra/mate.htm

Geoliteracy and Freedom Schools

Literacy and education for liberation have always been important themes within Black community spaces. The Freedom

School model was designed to transform communities by helping people to recognize their collective strengths and to exercise their political power. In this sense, the Freedom School concept aligns with the mate masie Adinkra symbol shown in Figure 12.2, emphasizing the importance of internalizing knowledge. In the modern context, Freedom Schools serve the vital function of emphasizing the connection between education and freedom. Annually, tens of thousands of students (referred to as scholars in the program) participate in Freedom Schools sponsored by schools, churches, and nonprofit organizations. These scholars are routinely introduced to literature and learning, highlighting how Black people have used education to pursue freedom.

They Learned Under the Trees

Freedom Schools emerged during the era of the 1960s' Black Freedom movement. They were temporary schools that offered Black children supplemental learning and emboldened young people critically to question the world in which they lived. A distinctive aspect of Freedom Schools was their resistance to racist schooling systems that went to great lengths to maintain the status quo and worked to keep Black students down. The Black students who attended the different variations of Freedom Schools were unbowed. They learned under trees, in makeshift community centers, and in church basements. They could be found in locations such as the Arkansas Delta; the Mississippi Delta; Boston; Selma, Alabama; and Farmville, Virginia. Freedom Schools are a historical but sometimes forgotten testament to emancipatory Black education. One of the most identifiable Freedom Schools examples can be found during the 1964 Mississippi Summer Project (also known as the Freedom Summer), the Student Nonviolent Coordinating Committee (SNCC), and other civil rights organizations enacted.

Freedom Summer not only still stands as one of the pivotal moments in breaking through well-entrenched racism but also provides a glaring model for what can happen when local people and, more importantly, youth engage in mass organizing. The SNCC Freedom Schools curriculum and structure as a model for Black children's emancipatory education is a redemptive feature of the Black Freedom movement that is still relevant today.

I Can Make a Difference in my World.
The Children's Defense Fund (CDF) Freedom Schools are a contemporary reiteration of the 1964 Freedom Schools. The program is focused on literacy, civic engagement, and social action, and the curriculum spans kindergarten through 12th grade. The overarching theme of the CDF Freedom Schools curriculum is "I Can Make a Difference." Each week of the program focuses on six subthemes that allow youth participants to explore their ability to make a difference in self, family, community, country, world, and hope, education, and action. Within the Freedom Schools curriculum, geoliteracy is most visible in the subtheme of "I Can Make a Difference in My World." The subtheme's goal for making a difference in the world is to help scholars explore the world and how their stories connect with others around the globe. Stories about African people and culture around the world are explored through books such as the following:

- *Anansi the Spider: A Tale from the Ashanti* (McDermott, 1972)

- *Beatrice's Goat* (McBrier, 2001)

- *Desmond and the Very Mean Word* (Tutu & Abrams, 2013)

- *I and I: Bob Marley* (Medina, 2009)

- *Masai and I* (Kroll, 1992)

- *The Girl Who Buried Her Dreams in a Can: A True Story* (Trent, 2015)

- *Tutankhamen's Gift* (Sabuda, 1994)

- *14 Cows for America* (Deedy, 2009)

Alongside reading the books, students are engaged in cooperative learning activities such as role-playing, poetry, artwork, graphic organizers, social action, and conflict resolution that bring the stories to life. This approach is intended to help the scholars keep the Diaspora's wisdom and knowledge beyond their summer in the program.

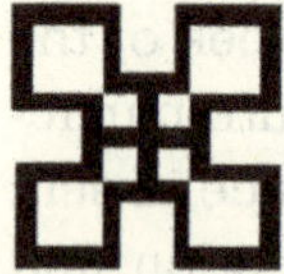

Figure 12.3. *Nsaa*—one who does not know authentic nsaa (cloths) will buy fakes (meaning: excellence, genuineness, authenticity) *Source:* http://www.adinkra.org/htmls/adinkra/nsaa.htm

Geoliteracy and Global Black Arts Movements

Despite the serious need, very little learning about the arts and world geography is offered to Black students in U.S. schools. Research on culturally informed understanding has shown that regular and consistent exposure to cultural arts learning opportunities has a profound positive impact on students. Education researchers have identified five important elements of culturally responsive education:

- Cultural literacy

- Self-reflective analysis of one's beliefs

- Caring

- Trusting and inclusive classrooms, respect for diversity

- A transformative curriculum

These five elements reflect excellence and authenticity individually and collectively, the cultural meanings connected to the nsaa Adinkra symbol shown in Figure 12.3. Next, we reflect on (1) experiences from an afterschool literacy and creative arts curriculum and program that Professor Kazembe created and (2) the role of geoliteracy within the curriculum and the facilitation.

Using Global Black Arts Movements to Elevate Black Children's Learning

elev8te is a literacy and creative arts program that introduces participants to the cultural, historical, and political impact of the six Global Black Arts Movements mentioned later. Explicitly designed for elementary school-age students, elev8te introduces them to a nearly century-long tradition of Black arts and artists (i.e., writers, poets, visual and performing artists) who developed and used art to transform themselves and society. The program introduces Black students to culturally and historically significant art, music, and literature developed within the Global Black Arts Movements.

Spanning nearly a century, Global Black Arts Movements represented an exciting Black creative expression and cultural development period. During the 20th century, Black writers, poets, visual, and performing artists established six crucial historical, social, and cultural movements that flourished in the United States, Europe, Africa, and the Caribbean. Known as *Global Black Arts Movements*, they included the following:

- Indigéniste (Haiti)

- Négrismo (Cuba and Puerto Rico)

- Négritude (Paris, French Guiana, Martinique)

- New Negro Movement/Harlem Renaissance (New York)

- Black Chicago Renaissance (Chicago)

- Black Arts Movement (United States)

Global Black Arts Movements linked Black artists-activists in international campaigns for freedom and liberation. Black intellectuals and artists developed and used art to mount campaigns of resistance, social justice, education, and cultural expression.

Geoliteracy is an important component of the elev8te program. During the first segment of the six-part program, students learn about Indigéniste, the artistic movement developed in Haiti during the 1920s and 1930s. Haitian writers, artists, and activists of that period understood the word *Indigéniste* as referring to their search for their *Blackness or African identity*. Students can make an immediate, authentic connection between the search for identity among Haitians and African Americans. As students learn about the writers and activists who developed the Indigéniste movement, they also study maps and country history. During this component of the program, students learn about Haiti's physical location and its proximity and importance to other areas of the African Diaspora.

Geoliteracy is further emphasized in the students' learning about the poetry/poets/poetics of the Global Black Arts Movements. For example, as students read poetry from the Négrismo movement (the artistic and social movement that evolved in Cuba and Puerto Rico during the 1920s), they learn how to pronounce and identify geoliteracy sight words and cultural terms such as *peasant*, *fiesta*, and *El Morro*. When students encounter these words, they are automatically linked to a particular place in the world (Cuba or Puerto Rico), a particular era (the postcolonial period), and a particular people (Afro-Cubans). Additionally, teaching geoliteracy skills enables students to make an instant connection to particular historical/political contexts (e.g., the struggle against enslavement and imperialism; the search for and celebration of African identity and Black cultural expression).

When students develop geoliteracy skills, they become more globally connected, informed, and active. Geoliteracy provides a gateway for students to acquire the deep learning and robust skills that are so critical in today's world.

Figure 12.4. *akoma ntoso*—"linked hearts" (agreement and understanding)
Source: http://www.adinkra.org/htmls/adinkra/akon.htm

Conclusion

When the cultural meaning of the akoma ntoso (see Figure 12.4) is activated, we all benefit from mutual agreement and understanding. We have discussed two different education programs (Freedom Schools and elev8te) and described how each contributes to enriching and expanding Black students' educational possibilities. Geoliteracy is an important feature of both curricula as it is designed to challenge and enhance the way students understand and see the world. By expanding their understanding of *where* African people are, students understand *who* African people are. Geoliteracy is crucial to Black students' education because it encourages them to develop a broader lens on African people's culture, experiences, and shared history throughout the world. In turn, this expanded view allows Black students to gain insight and inspiration by studying and seeing the deep cultural interconnections among and between people sprinkled throughout the African Diaspora.

With the police murder of George Floyd in Minneapolis during the summer of 2020, we entered a new phase of racial protest uprising and struggle for liberation. One of the key questions that continues to be raised is "What do we tell our children?" For long decades, Freedom Schools have functioned as sites of community discourse and models for education, democratic engagement, and community transformation. Those who create, teach in, and support Freedom Schools regard them as important vehicles for Black children and youth's education.

The optimal and holistic development of Black children is a prominent feature within and across both models that we have discussed. Within these alternative learning settings, Black students engage in rich discussions and learning experiences about identity, power, culture, and history. Unlike traditional educational contexts, the Freedom Schools and elev8te models provide students with a strong foundation and context to understand difficult subjects such as racial violence, imperialism, and colonization. Both models emphasize the resilience, heritage, and enormous diversity of African ancestry people both in the United States and throughout the world.

References

Deedy, C. A. (2009). *14 cows for America*. Peachtree Publishing Company.

Kroll, V. (1992). *Masai and I*. Aladdin.

McBrier, P. (2001). *Beatrice's goat*. Aladdin.

McDermott, G. (1972). *Anansi the spider: A tale from the Ashanti*. Henry Holt & Company.

Medina, T. (2009). *I and I: Bob Marley*. Lee & Low Books.

Sabuda, R. (1994). *Tutankhamen's gift*. Aladdin.

Trent, T. (2015). *The girl who buried her dreams in a can: A true story*. Viking Books for Young Readers.

Tutu, D., & Abrams, D. C. (2013). *Desmond and the very mean word*. Candlewick Press.

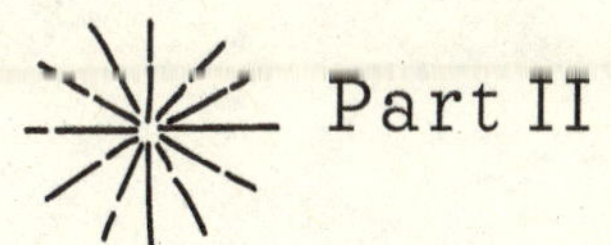 Part II

BLACK FOLKS ALL OVER THE WORLD

13

Dr. Clement T. M. Lambert

African Diaspora Literacy in Jamaica and the Wider Caribbean

Jamaica: An Introduction

Nestled in the Western Caribbean between Cuba and Hispaniola is Jamaica—the largest English-speaking nation in the Caribbean. With a population of under 3 million, about 92% of the residents are of African descent. Jamaica is famous for reggae music (Bob Marley), athletics (Usain Bolt), and pioneering intellectual thought on pan-Africanism (Marcus Garvey). Despite the rich heritage that runs deep in the Jamaican vein, it is a country of paradoxes and controversies related to African Diaspora Literacy.

Imagine an island of a little over 4,000 square miles with lush landscapes. Hills, valleys, plains, mountains, and beautiful beaches are all within an hour's ride. A country with rich religious roots as well as a voracious appetite for revelry, the unique cuisine is deeply influenced by African, European, and Asian ingredients and techniques. Jamaica is a country where politics and policies have shaped national development and the will of its people. The country's motto is "out of many one people," yet the Indigenous populations were totally decimated by European colonizers, and the European slave trade provided African slaves for centuries. Imagine a country trying to break from the colonial legacies that entailed brutality and prejudice but produced some of the most persistent and creative minds. Yes, you have imagined Jamaica—a country where Europeans first arrived in 1494 that Columbus described as the most beautiful isle he had ever seen. Like its Caribbean counterparts, when cane sugar was in its heyday Jamaica was the breadbasket for European colonizers. The actions of the colonizers shaped both the population and the economy of these islands for centuries. The colonial legacy of Jamaica includes genocide, slavery, and bloody slave revolts. Yet the official head of state of Jamaica is still Queen Elizabeth, and the country still boasts a Westminster-style government. Despite the colonial legacy of oppression and abuse, Jamaica's heritage also includes stories of creativity, unbridled talent, resistance, and triumph. One striking example is in the stories of Nanny of the Maroons—Jamaica's only national heroine who holds legendary status for her tactical triumphs over a well-equipped British army. Nanny, a famous Maroon warrior leader, fought across the "New World," including in South America, the United States, and the Caribbean. She is known for resistance to slavery via uprisings (Brown, 2020).

Schooling in Jamaica

Schooling and teaching in Jamaica began even before slavery ended in 1838. Enslavers' children typically went back to England to study. Some Jamaicans who were enslaved learned to read based on their status as "house slaves" and their interactions with their "masters." Others were taught to read by missionaries under the guise of converting them to Christianity. After slavery ended, many former slaves did not want to be connected with the memories of their forced and harsh work on sugar plantations. Despite their best efforts to resist, slavery and negative race relations have lingered in the Jamaican psyche for a long time.

Education became a very attractive pathway away from that route. Schools started through trust funds, churches, and eventually, the government began to educate the general population. Today, the education system has evolved in Jamaica, where universal education is mostly government-funded for children from kindergarten to 11th grade. The curriculum is government-designed and highly influenced by high-stakes examinations at various stages of schooling. Despite catering to over 90% of students from the African diaspora, this curriculum has little direct reference to African heritage, and teachers are not formally prepared to promote African Diaspora Literacy in schools.

Jamaican Perspectives

Jamaica often presents as the story of two countries. Kingston, the capital, was declared a cultural site by the United Nations in 2019. This honor was given because of many famous Jamaicans (including Bob Marley) and their contributions to the international cultural landscape. During apartheid in South Africa, Jamaican entertainers and even politicians were among the most vocal calling for an end to apartheid through song (e.g., "Free Mandela," "Can You?" among many others),[1] speeches, and boycotts. The Rastafarian religion, which emerged in Jamaica, had strong African perspectives and a very vocal "back to Africa" message. The Universal Negro Improvement Association, founded by Marcus Garvey, heralded the theme "Africa for Africans at home and abroad," also a strong back-to-Africa theme.

The "second" Jamaica entailed a rigid school system and policymakers who rejected the native Jamaican language (which has gone through several names—Patois, Jamaican Creole, and now Jamaican). The official language of instruction

---

1   Many more songs can be located by a simple Google search on Jamaican anti-apartheid songs.

is English, and Jamaican talk has only recently (around 2000) been acknowledged as the home language of over 90% of the children who attend schools. Jamaican, which is a combination of African and European languages, was designated as "bad talk" by educators and policymakers. Therefore, it lacked the sponsorship to be formalized as a language of instruction for Jamaican students. Jamaican creole is the dominant mode of communication for the mass of the people in the Caribbean (Bryan, 2010). Bryan (2010) cites a very heavy Twi (a dialect of the Akan language spoken mostly in south and central Ghana; "Twi," 2000) influence on the pronunciation, grammar, and vocabulary of the Jamaican language. She explains that Jamaican language also has roots in many different European and even Asian languages. Perhaps her most striking observation is that

> the most significant non-British category is the African. The African lexicon is significant and is used in all aspects of life but is especially numerous in plants, foods, utensils, music, dancing, superstition, people and their conditions, and greetings and exclamations. . . . A few examples include: ackee, pumpun, afu, yampee (plants); duckunu, janga, toto, busu (food); bankra, cotta (furnishings/utensils); ketta, abeng (music); jumbi, obeah (beliefs); bafan, yaw (ailments). . . . (Bryan, 2010, p. 11)

The work of cultural activists has also promoted the importance of Jamaican language and its linkages to our African roots. Louise Bennett ("Miss Lou"—a cultural icon) is very important in prompting and legitimizing Jamaican talk. Bennett was a Jamaican poet, performer, and cultural ambassador who pioneered the promotion of the Jamaican language in significant ways (Cooper, 2009).

Color has also been a dominant issue in Jamaica. While this has evolved, historically, a person of lighter complexion is more favorably considered in many circles. They had a better chance of being selected for certain jobs and even better relationships and marriage choices. This and other factors have led to the neglect of African heritage in formal and informal circles and to issues such as rampant skin bleaching. These factors have long pointed to the need for African Diaspora Literacy among the Jamaican population.

The Jamaican School Curriculum

The Jamaican school curriculum covers a wide range of subjects and tracks for school completion. In our primary schools (Grades 1–6), English language arts, mathematics, science, social studies, religious education, health and family life education, and civics, to a lesser extent, are included in the curriculum. A close examination of the Jamaican curriculum revealed references to the Jamaican heritage, but very little reference is made to Africa and our African heritage.

Teacher preparation (preservice and in-service) has not formally contributed to teacher awareness of or inclusion of African Diaspora Literacy in their instruction. I interviewed teachers from elementary schools across Jamaica, and they candidly described a situation that pointed to the need for African Diaspora Literacy for students, parents, and themselves as teachers. The teachers were candid in stating the term *African Diaspora Literacy* was very new to them. According to one teacher I call Terrylee,[2]

> Well, I have never heard it before but let me unpack it to see if I am on the right track. African Diaspora refers to persons of African descent around the world. Literacy, what I am looking at is, it is based on an Afrocentric perspective based on your understanding of your heritage and history.

---

2   Pseudonyms are used to protect the teachers' identity.

Denise, another teacher, stated,

> It means maybe like different African groups. . . . Maybe different African groups of people live in other countries—so their literacy is like learning about their cultural background.

The teachers quoted made good inferences regarding what African Diaspora Literacy might be. However, others offered erroneous explanations, including "the literacy rate of Africans."

Whatever definitions the Jamaican teachers gave regarding African Diaspora Literacy, our conversations pointed to the negative effects of Western education and perspectives and the need for a greater celebration of our African identity in Jamaican schools. According to Terrylee,

> I've been teaching for 12 years, and I've yet to see there's been just talk about integrating our history (more so the teachings of Marcus Garvey) in schools. It was done in the past, but for decades now, that has been tossed aside. So, every year we turn out students who are inundated with Americanized culture. And the aspects of that culture that are celebrated are not the aspects that speak to self-love as persons of African descent.

Denise poignantly points to the effects of Western perspectives which transcends student education and points to a profoundly rooted situation:

> Some of us as teachers are kind of enslaved, too, because as adults, some believe that if our nose no strait, we not pretty. We have to change our mindset as well to find importance in teaching those students. Because even though we talk

about it and we say we should love our Blackness and whatever, you have some persons you go on the road, and you see
persons of dark complexion. We exclaim at his Blackness
and often equate Blackness with ugliness. But if we see
a white person, we say, "Wow she is so pretty!" . . . If our
mindset is changed, even if it is not a part of the curriculum, we can do things that children will emulate to see, you
know, praise Black people. When you have the little Black
children at home, compliment their complexion instead of
saying, "How you so Black, gal?"

Effect of Western Education on Jamaican Children

Jamaica has mostly followed a Western model of education,
which has left deeply rooted implicit and explicit Western
values in Jamaican children's perspectives. Traditionally, the
curriculum lauded European "pioneers" who "discovered"
Jamaica and benevolent Europeans who saw to our freedom.
This has changed to a more balanced perspective over the
years. However, what has not received enough attention in the
formal education system is the systematic exploration of our
African heritage and promoting value and pride in this dimension that accounts for the heritage of the wider Jamaican and
Caribbean populations. Unfortunately, being "too Black" is still
perceived as a disadvantage in some Jamaican circles. This can
be attributed to the centuries of projecting Eurocentric images
in education and religious literature. While the tides are chang-
ing, Western education has disproportionately favored stories of European triumph and downplayed African greatness.
Marcus Garvey recognized this anomaly almost a century ago
when he declared, "A **people without** the knowledge of their
past history, origin and culture is like a tree **without** roots"
(Afrobella, 2009, emphasis added). This underscores the need
for African Diaspora Literacy then and even more so now. To

promote awareness and appreciation of self is important to include cultural knowledge (i.e., African history, religion, science, and philosophy) in the Jamaican school curriculum.

Recommendation for Families and Communities in Jamaica and the Caribbean

The formal school system has been moving too slowly toward promoting African Diaspora Literacy in Jamaica and the Caribbean. Therefore, parents and families need to take steps to enable this essential dimension as discussed in the following recommendations.

Public Awareness, Buy-In, and Advocacy

There are pockets in the Jamaican population that have valued and continue to promote our African heritage—not necessarily in the name of African Diaspora Literacy. The Bobo Ashanti community of Bull Bay ("Bobo Ashanti," 2020) and Liberty Hall, established by Marcus Garvey and evolved into a center for teaching and celebrating matters pertinent to the African Diaspora (Williams, 2019), are notable examples. However, these communities tend to be under-recognized within Jamaican education circles. Alliances between notable scholars (e.g., Boutte et al., 2017, 2018) and Jamaican advocates would add legitimacy to promoting African Diaspora Literacy in the Caribbean.

Caribbean families and communities can be instrumental in advocacy by lobbying local schools and governments through parent-teacher associations, media appearances, and other means to place greater emphasis on African Diaspora Literacy in schools.

Increasing Knowledge of African Diaspora Literacy

Caribbean families and communities need to know the importance of African Diaspora Literacy through essential readings, public lectures, and exploration of websites. Even a search of local newspapers on the topic might be useful. It is also essential to explore history books (e.g., Diptee, 2010) that provide a more balanced view of the transatlantic journey of Africans to the Western Hemisphere.

Jamaica and the wider Caribbean are on a quest to balance and further understand their intellectual, social, and cultural heritage. Greater attention to African Diaspora Literacy will prove to be an essential dimension of this journey.

Internet Resources

- O'Gilvie, D. (n.d.). *Ghana and Nigeria: Jamaica's not-so-distant relatives*. Griot's Republic. http://www.griotsrepublic.com/ghana-nigeria-jamaicas-not-distant-relatives/

- B:M20. (2020, June 27). *History of Jamaica*. https://www.blackhistorymonth.org.uk/article/section/jamaica/history-of-jamaica/

- Charles, C. A. D. (2003). Skin bleaching, self-hate and Black identity in Jamaica. *Journal of Black Studies, 33*(6), 711–728. https://citeseerx.ist.psu.edu/viewdoc/download?doi=10.1.1.895.8713&rep=rep1&type=pdf

- National Standards Curriculum of Jamaica:

  https://pep.moey.gov.jm/grades1-3-national-standards-curriculum/

  https://pep.moey.gov.jm/grades-4-6-national-standards-curriculum/

  https://pep.moey.gov.jm/grade-7-9-national-standards-curriculum/

- Lambert, C. (2019, September 5). *Is there an elephant in the room? Race, colour and our national heritage.*

Jamaica Observer. http://www.jamaicaobserver.com/opinion/is-there-an-elephant-in-the-room-race-colour-and-our-african-heritage_173686?profile=1097

References

Afrobella. (2009, August 17). *Remembering old Marcus Garvey*. http://www.afrobella.com/2009/08/17/remembering-old-marcus-garvey/

Bobo Ashanti. (2020, October 17). In *Wikipedia*. https://en.wikipedia.org/wiki/Bobo_Ashanti

Boutte, G., Johnson, G., & Muki, A. (2018). Revitalization of Indigenous African knowledges among people in the African Diaspora. In L. Johnson, G. Boutte, G. Greene, & D. Smith (Eds.), *African Diaspora Literacy, the heart of transformation in K-12 schools and teacher education* (pp. 13–42). Lexington Books.

Boutte, G., Johnson, G, Wynter-Hoyte, K., & Uyota, K. E. (2017). Using African Diaspora Literacy to heal and restore the souls of young black children. *International Critical Childhood Studies, 6*(1), 66–79. https://journals.sfu.ca/iccps/index.php/childhoods/article/viewFile/56/pdf

Brown, D. L. (2020, August 19). Kamala Harris's dad was from Jamaica, where a fierce woman warrior once fought slavery. *The Washington Post*. https://www.washingtonpost.com/history/2020/08/19/nanny-maroons-kamala-slavery-jamaica/

Bryan, B. (2010). *Between two grammars: Research and practice for language learning and teaching in a Creole-speaking environment*. Ian Randle Publishers.

Cooper, C. (2009). Pedestrian crosses: Sites of dislocation in "post-colonial" Jamaica. *Inter-Asia Cultural Studies, 10*(1), 3–11.

Diptee, A. (2010). *From Africa to Jamaica: The making of an Atlantic slave society, 1775–1807*. University Press of Florida. http://search.ebscohost.com.libproxy.nau.edu/login.aspx?direct= true&db=nlebk&AN=482942&site=ehost-live

Twi. (2020, October 25). In *Wikipedia*. https://en.wikipedia.org/wiki/Twi#
     :~:text=Twi%20(Akan%3A%20%5Bt%C9%95%E1%B6%A3i%5D,
     major%20ethnic%20groups%20in%20Ghana

Williams, P. H. (2019, December 26). *Liberty Hall hosts pre-Kwanzaa fest*. The
     Gleaner. http://jamaica-gleaner.com/article/news/20191226/liberty-
     hall-hosts-pre-kwanzaa-fest

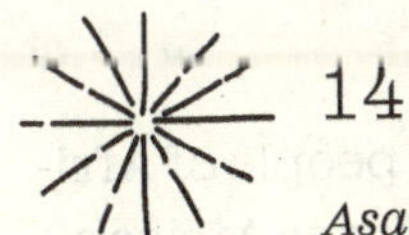

14

*Asangha Ngufor Muki, Samuel Ntewusu,
Moepeola Omoegun, and Berte Van Wyk*

Lessons From Africa

This chapter focuses on Africa and what we can learn to promote and advance the love of people of African descent worldwide. Promoting African Diaspora people's return to the continent is not a new idea. The early 20th century saw the rise of pan-African activist Marcus Garvey's "Back to Africa" movement, which sought greater Black social and economic independence. In recent years, many Black people have traveled to Africa to visit or have relocated there. The global recognition of the need to embrace Black people's humanity and collective destiny can be seen in many ways:

- The Black Lives Matter movement, https://blacklives matter.com/

- The United Nations' declaration of 2015–2024 as the International Decade for People of African Descent (Resolution 68/237) cites the need to strengthen national, regional, and international cooperation in relation to the full enjoyment of economic, social, cultural, civil, and political rights of people of African descent, and their full and equal participation in all aspects of society (United Nations, n.d.).

- In 2003, the African Union designated people of African origin who live outside the continent as Africa's Sixth Region (see Figure 14.1).

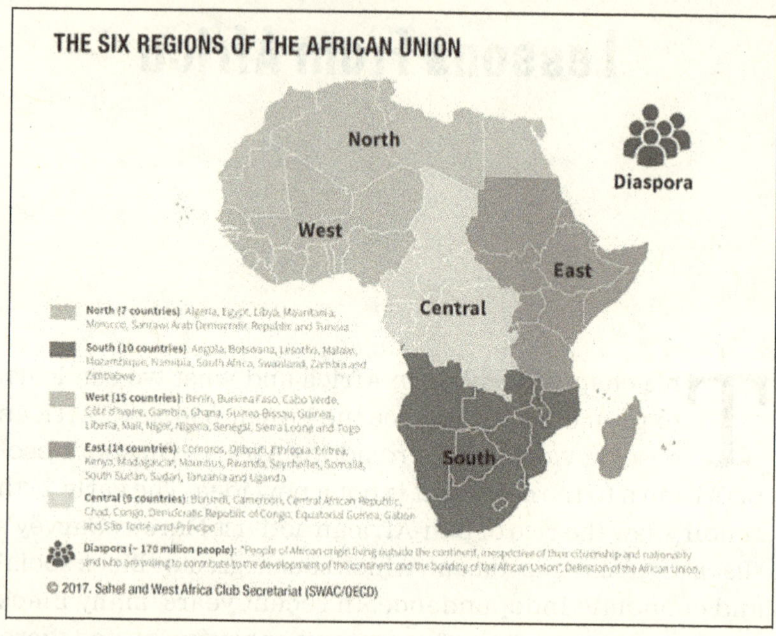

Figure 14.1. African Union
Source: https://stateofafricandiaspora.international/the-6th-region/. Used with permission.

This chapter explores lessons from three different African regions that can enhance the understanding of Africa's rich cultural heritage and showcase the continent as a beloved place not only to learn about but also to learn *from*. The first part of the chapter, by Asangha Muki, a native Cameroonian, brings an African perspective on "teaching children to be resilient, independent, and smart" focused on lessons from Cameroon in Central Africa. The second section of the chapter by Moepeola Omoegun, an indigene of Nigeria, discusses "African Indigenous and traditional education systems," focusing on lessons from Nigeria in West Africa. The third segment, by Samuel Ntewusu, includes lessons from Ghana, also in West Africa, focused on "teaching children about values using Adinkra symbols." The closing section by Berte Van Wyk from South Africa emphasizes "Indigenous Khoikhoi and San ways of knowing."

Lessons From Cameroon: Teaching Children to Be Resilient, Independent, and Smart

African instruction seeks to prepare students for adulthood. Indigenous pedagogies permit toddlers and youngsters to learn in participatory processes in the home, community, religious service, peer groups, and so forth through "work-play" activities, with little to no explicit instructional support (Nsamenang, 2008). "Child work" is a basic African cultural mode of preparing the next generation, and it is understood by both the family and the young as necessary for the family and for the youngsters' developmental learning. With Africa's traditions of "child work," children do tasks, even difficult ones, on their own.

In Cameroon, most children's "work" is undertaken in child-to-child sociability and with peer mentorship instead of with parents, other adults, or teachers. Peer cultures offer children opportunities to play, work, and learn together, free from parental supervision and adult control. Accordingly, the freedom of the peer culture breeds creativity and challenges children to cultivate prosocial values and altruism, defer to elders and more competent peers, address and resolve conflicts, and take the perspective to notice needs and serve them (Asangha, 2015; Nsamenang, 2008).

According to Fomba (2011), participatory teaching in Bali Nyonga, Cameroon, prepares youth for preparation in the labor market. Children are engaged in sustainable livelihood activities such as farming, carpentry, mechanics, craft, fishing, animal rearing, blacksmithing, and small businesses such as trading. Investment in life skills through traditional preparation strategies has been drawn from the firm belief that young people are agents of change with the potential of taking a leading role in the socioeconomic development of their communities as they transition from childhood to the world of work.

Likewise, according to Tchombe (2011), the Bamiléké child engages very early in various forms of interaction with persons and with available rich, meaningful physical and material resources. In some instances, adolescents are already the owners of a farm or a small business and a member of a "thrift and loan" or Njangi group, which is an avenue to raise capital through loans to start or sustain an existing business. Such meaningful, sustainable, and transferable experiences are fostered by inculcating the values of endurance, patience, persistence, honesty, respect, and hard work, which are indelible characteristics of the Bamiléké people of Cameroon. Perseverance, according to the people, is the key to success. In this culture, socio-affective development is the basis for developing the spirit of being socially competent (an important strand of resilient identity). These abilities, skills, and values are learned through farming and trading, the people's main economic activities. As they develop, children participate in economic activities depending on the nature and difficulty level of such tasks as selling, bargaining, and negotiating the prices of commercial wares.

What Can Black People Learn From Cameroonian Socialization of Children?

- Children are active participants in the socialization and learning process rather than just being passive recipients of adults' knowledge.

- Beginning with birth, children learn from and with parents, teachers, and adult community members.

Lessons From Nigeria: African Indigenous and Traditional Education Systems

Before British colonization, the African Indigenous system taught students practical skills to function successfully in traditional society. Usually, children 2 or 3 years of age belonged to an age group. Together, they learned the community's customs and were assigned specific duties around the village, such as sweeping lanes or clearing bush. As the children grew older, the boys were introduced to farming and more specialized work, such as wood carving or drumming. Girls would learn farming and domestic skills while boys would often enter into apprenticeship-type relations with master craftsmen. Even in the 21st century, this kind of education is expected. Examples of this can be seen in the children's book *One Big Family: Sharing Life in an African Village* (Onyefulu, 1999).

African Indigenous education is defined by Enueme (2006) as the traditional method, through which a society passes on its culture or way of life to its young ones and succeeding generations without any interference from other cultures. It is the original African way of transmitting the values and skills in a society without foreign influence at any stage or time to the young ones. Such African Indigenous education was highly advanced and included storytelling, folklores, mythologies, proverbs, songs, dance, and many other traditions (Omoegun, 2004).

In the traditional African setting, children are well valued and show each family's economic strength—especially in Nigeria. The birth of a child is usually celebrated, and names are given to highlight the significance of the child's birth. For example, there is a saying in Yoruba: *Olomo lo laiye*, meaning "those who have children have life." Names are given also to emphasize the religious faith and background of the family, such as "Ogunyemi," representing the god of iron that has beautified my life.

The newborn grew in a warm and loving environment right from birth, nurtured by the parents who provide home training, the first form of education. Such home training includes the cultural belief that everybody in the community has a say about the child's development. It is a collective responsibility to put the child on the right path and correct any misbehavior without asking for the parents' permission or consent.

In Nigeria, especially among the Southwest Yoruba-speaking group, storytelling used to be an avenue through which morals and societal values are taught from childhood to young adulthood. Such stories were usually narrated by the adults who were regarded as the residue of knowledge through their various life experiences. Children looked forward to the evenings when they would gather together to listen to "the tales by moonlight" in their various compounds.

What Can Black People Learn From Nigerian Education and Socialization?

- Children's names should be meaningful.

- We can teach values through storytelling, proverbs, and everyday activities.

- It is essential to respect elders, even if they are not blood relatives. Even today, children show respect for adults by addressing them as "auntie" and "uncle."

Lessons From Ghana: Teaching Children About Values Using Adinkra Symbols

Symbols stand for something visible. A symbol can be an object, a mark, a sign, or an abstract idea. When a child is born in Ghana, society begins to share its values with them through teaching, learning, and practice. Children are socialized into understanding society and the environment through symbols such as Adinkra symbols, which are traditional images in Ghana that are translations of thoughts and ideas in society. Adinkra is said to have originated from the name of a powerful African king in present-day Cote d'Ivoire. He was called Kofi Adinkra. In the 1800s, the Ashanti of Ghana incorporated Adinkra's art into their kingdom (Agbo, 2006). Two examples of the Adinkra symbols and their importance to children and society are discussed below.

The *Sankofa* symbol (Figure 14.2) is a bird whose body is facing forward with the head and neck looking backward. The symbol is as old as the existence of Black people. In the tombs and walls of ancient Kemet in present-day Egypt, a version of the Sankofa symbol can be found. It explains the human experience. As we go forward to the future, we also need to draw on lessons from the past. As we grow up, we do not need to abandon our ancestors' cultural traditions and values. As we face modernity, these values are also crucial in our lives since they can guide us.

Elders in Ghana often include references to Sankofa to let the children know about it and its importance. It is appropriate for an adult to tell a child, "You have made a mistake by doing A or B." The elder will conclude in Akan, "Sankofa yen Chi" (If you go back for it, it is not a taboo). The essence is to tell the child not to repeat that mistake the next time or to go back and do the right thing. Artists and members of the community also teach children to produce some of the Adinkra symbols as a pastime. The ability to make the symbols usually on calabashes, cloth, or just even painting or drawing them on objects enables the children to have a permanent register of the symbol's meanings and importance.

Figure 14.2. Sankofa Adinkra symbol, which means "go back for it"
Source: http://www.adinkra.org/htmls/adinkra/sank.htm

The *funtunfunefu* (*fu-ntu-nfu-nafu*; Figure 14.3) symbol is two Siamese crocodiles. The symbol defines the relevance of different views in society. The message conveys to children that they can express divergent views, but they are also reminded that such views must be geared toward building consensus in the end—for the betterment of society. The symbol also teaches children about the unity of purposes and the strength in unity. For example, the conjoined crocodiles have one stomach. So even though they feed separately, the food goes into one stomach. In Ghana, the symbols teach children in the community to understand that while they are individuals, they also need to work toward the community's collective good.

Figure 14.3. Funtunfunefu-denkyemfunefu (Siamese crocodiles)—a symbol of democracy and unity. "The Siamese crocodiles share one stomach, yet they fight over food." This popular symbol is a reminder that infighting and tribalism are harmful to all who engage in it.
Source: http://www.adinkra.org/htmls/adinkra/funt.htm

Usually, when a community member requests support on his farm, the elderly people take the children along. The reason is to let the children understand the way society works—especially on issues that demand collective intervention.

Right from the beginning, the children see themselves first as community members before seeing themselves as individuals. The funtunfunefu symbol also helps children appreciate from the very onset the way and manner democratic systems work, especially in their ability to debate or express their views and how such debates can lead to achieving a common objective.

Lessons From the Symbols to Black People Worldwide

Sankofa reminds Black people to hold on to their values and go back to their cultural practices that have proven to be very important for their survival and relevance. Funtufunafu tells Black people that diversity is not an excuse for disunity. Whether we find ourselves in Africa, North and South America, or the Caribbean, we come from "one stomach," born of the same color and facing the same problems—marginalization. We must therefore harness our diverse skills to achieve unity and progress.

Lessons from South Africa: Indigenous Khoikhoi and San Ways of Knowing

The Khoikhoi and San people of South Africa have always been known for their strong understandings and ways of living. Indeed, the Dutch and English were well aware of the great strength that existed among Khoikhoi and San people. For example, Lord Macaulay, in his address to the British Parliament on February 2, 1835, commented,

> I have traveled across the length and breadth of Africa and have not seen one person who is a beggar, who is a thief such wealth I have seen in the country [South Africa], such high morals values, people of such caliber, that I do not think we would ever conquer this country unless we break the very backbone of this nation, which is her spiritual; and cultural heritage and therefore, I propose that we replace

her old and ancient education system, her culture, for if the Africans think that all that is foreign and English is good and greater than their own, they will lose their self-esteem, their native culture and they will become what we want them, a truly dominate nation. (Mogoeng, 2017, p. 4)

Like other African countries, when the Dutch and English "colonized" South Africa, they suppressed our Indigenous languages. English not only became one of the media of instruction but also the dominant one (the other being Afrikaans) up till today, and Indigenous cultures had to be learned in foreign-language classes. My own experience is that I grew up in a rural area where I heard a lot of communication in my Indigenous language, but that language was suppressed by the apartheid government.

While Indigenous Khoikhoi and San languages have never been recognized as official languages, they are constitutionally recognized. The current constitution recognizes the historically diminished use and status of the Indigenous languages of our people and acknowledges that the state must take tactical and positive measures to elevate the status and advance the use of these languages.

On a positive note, local communities started to revive Indigenous languages over the last 26 years that are now formally taught in some South African schools. As a result, new books are being produced in these languages. We recognize that language development continues to be closely intertwined with and inseparable from cultural identities (Cele, 2004, p. 42). Finally, language is not just language but is related to people's emotional and identity-construction.

What Can Be Learned From Khoikhoi and San People?

African people all over the world can gain insights from Khoikhoi and San people. Three lessons include the following:

- African people must recognize and reclaim their Indigenous cultural strengths.

- We should learn and use our Indigenous languages.

- We must be careful not to let European ways dominate our ways of being and understanding.

All three of these insights are important if we are to heal ourselves as African people.

Conclusion

These lessons from Africa are important for Black people wherever we are—on the continent and in the Diaspora. African traditional practices of assigning social responsibility to young people from an early age, based on African Indigenous knowledge systems, remain relevant for contemporary education goals in Africa and elsewhere. At best, this practice can serve as a context for learning about arts, values, health, and nutrition; fostering the importance of cooperation and nurturing support of others; and contributing to peaceful coexistence in society.

In many African societies, children's participation in family work is vital for developing social responsibility—an important dimension of intelligence. Work and play are better understood as complementary dimensions of activity than as separate activities. Cooperation with peers can be mobilized as a resource for co-constructive learning. Strategic opportunities for countering systemic bias in educational systems include focusing on African knowledges and languages in the curriculum and instruction.

References

Agbo, H. A. (2006). *Values of Adinkra and Agama symbols*. Bigshy Designs.

Asangha, M. N. (2015). Peer group activities and resilient identity among mid adolescents (15–17 years old): Case of Mbengwi sub division. *The African Journal of Special Education, 3*(1), 157–164.

Cele, N. (2004). 'Equity and diversity' and 'equity outcomes' challenged by language policy, politics and practice in South African higher education: The myth of language equality in education. *South African Journal of Higher Education, 18*(1), 38–56.

Enueme, C. P. (2006). *Education in Nigeria: A historical perspective.* Chambers Communication Ventures.

Fomba, E. M. (2011). Community role/engagement in vocational competence development. In A. B. Nsamenang & M. T. Tchombe (Eds.), *Handbook of African educational theories and practices: A generative teacher education curriculum* (pp. 518–528). HDRC.

Mogoeng, M. (2017, April 24). *Opening remarks* [Conference presentation]. Fourth Congress of the Conference of Constitutional Jurisdictions of Africa, Cape Town, South Africa.

Nsamenang, A. B. (2002). Adolescence in sub-Saharan Africa: An image constructed from Africa's triple inheritance. In B. B. Brown, R. W. Larson, & T. S. Saraswathi (Eds.), *The world's youth: Adolescence in eight regions of the globe* (pp. 61–104). Cambridge University Press.

Nsamenang, A. B. (2008). Agency in early childhood learning and development in Cameroon. *Contemporary Issues in Early Childhood Development, 9*(3), 211–223.

Omoegun, O. M. (2004): *My story book in values for the Nigerian child.* Literamed Publications.

Onyefulu, I. (1999). *One big family: Sharing life in an African village.* Gardners Press.

Tchombe, T. M. (2011). Cultural strategies for cognitive enrichment in learning among the Bamiléké of west region of Cameroon. In A. B. Nsamenang & M. T. Tchombe (Eds.), *Handbook of African educational theories and practices: A generative teacher education curriculum* (pp. 205–216). HDRC.

United Nations. (n.d.). *International decade for people of African descent.* https://www.un.org/en/observances/decade-people-african-descent

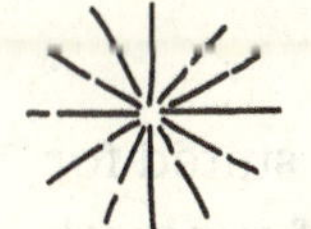

15

*Safi Darden, Melody Kuziwa Jombe, Wahida Sussex
and Ayanna Page*

We Be Schoolin'.
We Be Schooled:
Learning Across Educator
Partnerships with Youth
Voices at the Center

Introduction

In this chapter we reflect on a partnership for change between a higher education institution and two high schools (education for ages 11-16) in South West England, UK. The four authors are all women (two female university professors who immigrated to the UK—Safi and Melody) and two British high school staff specializing in student support (Wahida and Ayanna). We are all women of color, collectively with ancestry spanning Africa, Asia, the Caribbean, Europe and North America (Safi—Black American and Danish; Melody—Black African; Ayanna—Black Caribbean and English; and Wahida—South Asian British). We emphasize the importance of networks like this one for Black youth in majority white schools and a focus on reciprocal learning between youth and partners (us and our institutions).

Following an oral tradition was particularly suited for this group of partnership leaders and the focus of our work and this chapter is the result of a recorded and transcribed discussion amongst the four of us. We work in predominantly white institutions in a predominantly white European geographical region. We understand the importance of educational belonging and critical consciousness raising for our young Black students and the value of extracurricular activities. In our partnership, we work under the heading 'B-HUGs' (Black Heritage University Groups) and run in-school and outside of school (both during school hours) activities for Black youth aged 11–15 years old (see Figure 15.1 for the framing of program components and Table 15.1 for a description of the activities). We visualize our partnership activities within programme components termed "Butterfly Initiatives," a phrase coined by one of our Jegna. Each component stems from our learning and has unique aspects. Young people may engage with just one or with several components and rather than occurring in a linear fashion, at any point the components might intersect. These activities were supported by a collective of Jegna[1] who form a community brimming with Black excellence and dedication to supporting our youth and to an Afrocentric approach.

---

1   **Jegna (Jegnoch pl., Amharic):** A person who has faced adversity, has demonstrated determination and courage in the protection of their people, land, and culture, who produces exceptionally high-quality work and who dedicates themselves to the defense, nurturing, and development of young people by advancing their people, place, and culture. We have borrowed the application of this term from our Sisters at Guardians of Heritage.

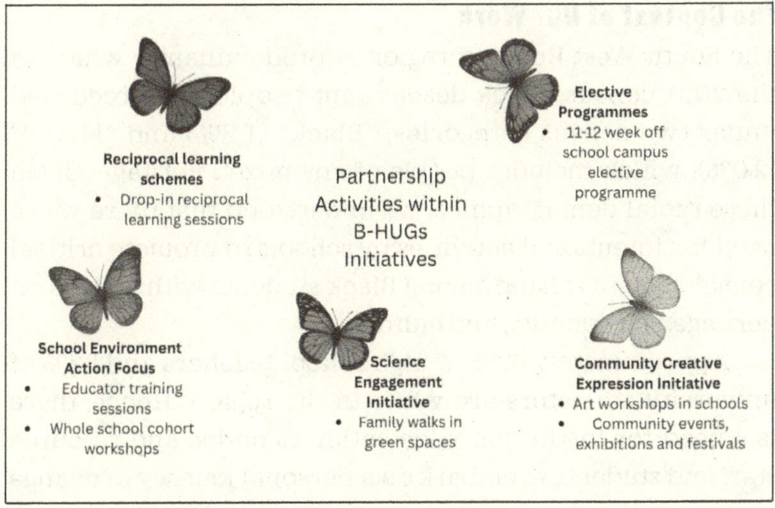

Figure 15.1. B-HUGs Program Components

Table 15.1. Description of BHUGs Partnership Activities Mapped in Figure 15.1.

Art workshops in schools with local Black artists, combining critical discussions of Black history with exploration of visual arts techniques, culminating in collaborative mixed-media pieces.

11-12 week elective program held on university campuses, blending group project work, creative activities, and Jegna-led workshops on topics such as self-advocacy and moral cognition.

Drop-in reciprocal learning sessions in schools with junior Jegna, offered in both one-to-one and group formats.

Family walks in green spaces to collect photographs, exchange stories across generations, and reflect on shared content.

Community events, exhibitions, and festivals curated by participating young people, showcasing their work and that of Black youth across the wider region.

Educator training sessions for critical consciousness raising, using youth-voice-centred materials.

Whole school cohort workshops designed to promote critical consciousness raising.

The Context of Our Work

The South West England region is predominantly white. In the 2021 census, Black descendant people were recorded under two census categories, "Black" (1.2%) and "Mixed" (2.0%), which includes people of any mixed heritage. Given these racial demographics, we understood that there was a need for intentional activities by schools to promote critical consciousness raising among Black students with a focus on heritage, self-identity, and culture.

Approximately 92% of high school teachers and 82% of university educators are white in the region. Hence, there is a need for institution-wide action to entice and resource staff and students to embark on a personal journey of change rooted in taking ownership of what they do not know—such as how to discuss race in the classroom—and doing the work to find out what they do not know.

Our Partnership

We acknowledge those who came before us and the reciprocal nature of action and the interconnectedness of humanity. We declare that the origin story of this partnership is infinite in its versions. Our own contributions to its *origin* in our positions as women of color, with a diversity of Black ancestry and migration stories, are not centred in this section. Rather we focus on a version of the origin of this partnership that travels through a single young person, Shafiqa, a Black girl in a predominantly white geographical region, at a predominately white school, with no Black teachers. We shared this story between us in our discussion, reinforcing the lore and offering the detail that each of us knew. Shafiqa spoke up and made her case for change. She voiced concern over lack of representation in the school environment, which was contributing to a negative experience of being in education. She challenged the leadership to take action on her behalf, and they did. They looked outside the institution for opportunities to engage Black students with Black educators—in a predominantly white geographical region, an institution of higher education just down the road, where Safi and Melody are based, was a good place to start. We hope that one day Shafiqa will know what the impact of her using her voice has been.

Partnership Foundation

The four of us (Safi, Melody, Ayanna, and Wahida) share a focus on taking action for change in the lives and education of Black youth and centering their voices. We envision ourselves as a protective circle around them. At the foundation of our partnership is trust, communication, and an intentional effort to understand each other's roles. We try to understand our scope, limitations, flexibility, good days, bad days, resources, authority, autonomy, reach, and capacity to influence, change, and effect institutional politics. Upon reflection, these are all reciprocal processes and are at the center of our partnership interventions, which are co-created within the *B-HUGs Model* (see Table 15.2). The work we do as B-HUGs focuses on collaborative and reciprocal learning and allows us to plan and implement ideas at pace and look after each other's well-being. We have developed the *B-HUGs Model* over a nearly two-year period and continue to build on it.

We are all bound by the Zulu proverb *"umuntu ngumuntu ngabantu!"* which directly translates to *I am because we are*. It carries the philosophy of Ubuntu, emphasising that our humanity is defined through our relationships with others, community, compassion, and interconnectedness.

Table 15.2. How We Approach Our Work

Our ***B-HUGs Model*** **for the work** rests on four interconnected pillars. While still a work in progress, this model reflects how we currently conceptualize our approach:

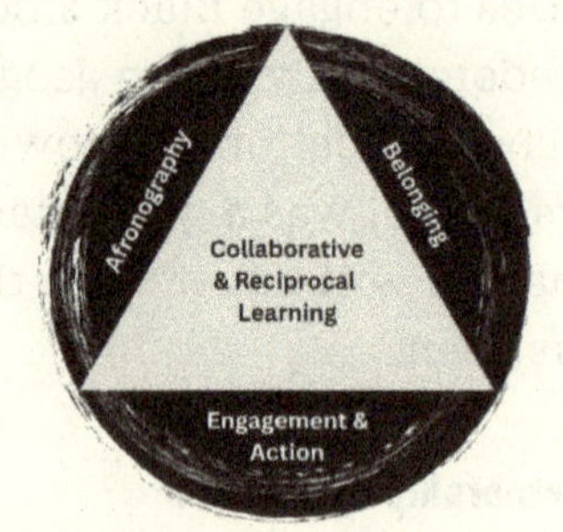

- **Collaborative and reciprocal learning** (core principle): We intentionally work outside a learning hierarchy.

- **Afronographic approach:** Understanding African culture, history, and heritage from an Afrocentric perspective.

- **Action and engagement:** Creating meaningful opportunities and fostering and taking action.

- **Belonging:** Creating and fostering spaces of belonging for Black youth and communities.

Note. Illustration depicts the B-HUGs model with "collaborative and reciprocal learning" at the center and three surrounding pillars: Afronographic approach, fostering action and engagement, and creating spaces of belonging.

Reflecting on the Value of the Partnership and its Ripples

Reflecting on the purpose of our work with Black youth, Wahida captured an expression of the value of the partnership in her diary entry below.

> **Diary Entry – 09-JUL-2025 – A Day at B-HUGs**
> The bell rings and they arrive
> bright eyes, eager hands,
> counting themselves in with high-fives with me.
> For a moment, the weight of home,
> the noise of school,
> is left at the door.
> Here, they are safe.
> Here, they are family.
> I watch them
> fed, nourished,

empowered until they stand taller.
They leave with knowledge stitched into their bones,
wearing it like capes.
Superheroes in their own right.
Each week brings a new adventure:
lawyers one week,
scientists the next.
Even lessons on how to stand unshaken
in the mirror of the "mainstream."
But we know the truth
they are the heartbeat of this enrichment,
the very reason it thrives.
When the day closes,
they line up.
Hugs are exchanged,
scrapbooks tucked under arms,
a little sadness hanging in the air
but fire glowing in their bellies,
ready for what comes next.
I smile.
I ask them, "How was today?"
And their laughter spills into buses,
into taxis,
into the streets
a chorus of joy,
a promise that they are ready,
so ready,
to take on the world

Additional value generated by our partnership comes from the 'ripple' it creates—which has been both unexpected and a force for growth, which came out resolutely in our discussion. Even before we ran any activities, we found that we were engaging young Black university students who applied for the roles we created to support this work. Having the opportunity to apply for a position on a project specific to supporting Black youth resonated so strongly that we drew interest from the full array of majors—arts and humanities to medicine to science, technology, engineering and maths. We saw true passion, commitment, and need for this work in each interview that we did. Our observations in the discussion often lingered on the bridge that these 'junior Jegna' that work on the project form between (senior) Jegna in the collective and their youngers in high school and on the new initiatives that we could bring to the work, such as in-school reciprocal learning sessions with junior Jegna and small groups of high school students. This could also work to further support our action for positive education experiences of young Black people in different stages of education at predominantly white institutions.

In another acknowledgement of the "ripple," Ayanna, who grew up in the same predominantly white region as our students, brought into discussion a section of a poem she wrote while in secondary school—a poem where she voiced her frustration with the stereotypes imposed on her. The poem itself stands as evidence of how reciprocal learning can be healing, the space the partnership created offered Ayanna the chance to heal in reciprocity with the students we were working with, "B-HUGs has definitely helped heal this part of me."

Lookin' back - I seen what done heal'd

If I was not mixed . . .
My hair wouldn't be subjected to unsolicited touch,
I wouldn't be a man's experimental date,
The sly joke during slavery history lessons,
A dancer of some kind,
Unsurprisingly fatherless,
And the predominately white institution's favourite diversity card.
That's how I know I'm mixed.

Importantly, young people and each of the partner institutions and staff carry along their own sets of expertise and resources, and in our discussion we found that we started to pull these together to make a plan for cross-institutional staff training centered on student voice. Without the partnership, this would not happen.

Challenges

Through our discussion it became clear that there were two main challenges: 1) we had not yet engaged parents/guardians; and 2) our interventions are sensitive to changes to institutional structure, policy, and resourcing; thus, we must build in resilience. In addition, we agreed that growing the scale of our work, the number of young people we engage, needs to be done with care as we may risk losing reciprocity in learning. In facing this challenge, we aim to diversify what we do—add to the activities in Table 15.1—and commit to working with small cohorts for each type of activity.

More Direct Messages from the Young People

So what do the young people we work with have to say more directly? In one of our *B-HUGs Elective Programmes* and one of our *B-HUGs Art Workshops* students expressed positive thoughts about: 1) belonging and empowerment; 2) joy, community, and connection; 3) heritage and culture; and 4) creative approaches. Quotes which represent participants' reflections on the B-HUGs elective and art workshops can be seen in Table 15.3.

Importantly, we are listening to what young people have voiced as outcomes they would like to see and what they would like to do more of. They want to bring learning to peers and teachers at school, an action we planned at various points of our discussion and formulated plans for further whole cohort work, teacher training, and supporting young people in creating school assemblies. They want to spend more time learning about and celebrating Black hair, culture, heritage, food, languages, music, and history through sharing—learning from each other. This reflection from young people was reiterated in other ways in terms of wanting additional sessions per week (e.g. Saturdays) and wanting to take the elective again, do more art workshops, and also in our own discussion on the limitation of time that we have for engagement, particularly as we are working within the school day for the majority of our activities. Young people also want us to increase the size of the partnership by adding more schools as the connection across schools was important to many.

Table 15.3. Themes and Illustrative Quotes from Youth Participants

Themes	Sample Quotes
Belonging and Empowerment	"(I)t's like really empowering to Black students, as they know that there's an elective for them." "I felt like I actually belong here. I don't feel like I belong in school but here, I have a place where I really belong."
Joy, Community, and Connection	"I have made a lot of friends which is so amazing." "It's a really fun elective, you learn more, and you get to engage with other schools and other people."
Heritage and Culture	Prompt: *Would you recommend B-HUGs elective to a friend and explain your answer?* Response: "Yes, they can learn more about Black culture and other things like how to take care of their hair . . . they can see how Black culture is like all over the world." Prompt: *What would you like to learn more about?* Response: "Everyone's identity."
Creative Approach	"I really like the workshop because it builds confidence with people inspiring them to be creative and social and how we had to paint and have fun with other people and I think many people should also experience this workshop for more social skills and love for their culture." "The project helped me and a lot of people to express culture and ideas."

Concluding Remarks: Building Futures, Shaping Change

Our partnership shows that centering Black students' voices, fostering belonging, and working collectively across institutions can generate ripples of change in even the most predominantly white contexts. The young people remind us that joy, creativity, and cultural pride are not extras but necessities for educational equity. By listening deeply, acting with reciprocity, and embracing Ubuntu, we can build spaces where Black heritage students thrive, schools transform, and communities connect. The challenge now is to sustain, resource, and expand this work so that every Black child feels seen, valued, and empowered in education.

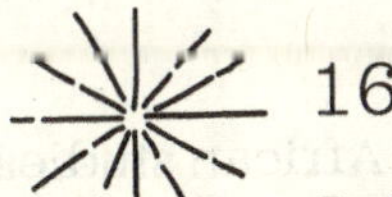

16

*LaGarrett J. King, Gloria Swindler Boutte,
Joyce E. King, George L. Johnson, Jr., and
Jarvais J. Jackson*

Resources

Throughout the book, authors have provided resources that affirm Black culture and identity. As we conclude, we provide additional resources that will help sustain loving spaces for Black children.

Our first recommended resource is *HomeTeam History*. *Hometeam History* was created to advance historical perspectives concerning African history, culture, and worldview. *Hometeam History* has a YouTube page of African-centered animated videos for school-aged children. The videos help students learn and relearn about African people's humanity and agency.

- HomeTeam History: https://www.youtube.com/@home teamhistory806

Other YouTube pages about Africa:

- Afrofoodtv: https://www.youtube.com/user/Afro FoodTV

- The Africa Channel: https://www.youtube.com/c/theafricachanneltv/videos

Our second recommendation consists of African studies programs housed at several universities and the Association for the Study of the Worldwide African Diaspora. Both offer internet resources and teaching tips for teachers and parents.

- The University of Pennsylvania's Arts and Sciences K–12 Internet Resources on Africa: http://www.africa.upenn.edu/outreach/k-12

- African Studies Center through the Boston University Pardee School of the Global Studies Department: http://www.bu.edu/africa/outreach/teachingresources/

- African Studies Program, University of Wisconsin: https://africa.wisc.edu/outreach-materials/

- African Studies Center, Michigan State University: https://africa.isp.msu.edu/program/outreach/k-12-programs/

- Center for African Studies, Howard University: https://cfas.howard.edu/about

- Kansas African Studies Center, University of Kansas: http://kasc.ku.edu/lesson-plans

- Indiana University Bloomington African Studies Program: https://africanstudies.indiana.edu/index.html

- Association for the Study of the Worldwide African Diaspora: http://aswadiaspora.org/

- Black Education Research Center: https://www.tc.columbia.edu/berc/

- USC Race and Equity Center: https://race.usc.edu

Third, we recommend a cultural resource center, Black homeschooling organization, and professional organizations focused on Black children and history.

- The IKG Cultural Resource Center: https://ikgcultural resourcecenter.com/mission-history/

- National Black Home Educators (NBHE): https://www. nbhe.net/

- National Association of Black School Educators (NABSE): https://nabse.org/about/our-mission/

- Association for the Study of African American Life and History (ASALH®): https://asalh.org/about-us/

- National Black Child Development Institute (NBCDI): https://www.nbcdi.org/

Our fourth recommendation includes books that explain the importance of teaching Black children about African heritage. Check Black bookstores (see the list in the following section) for copies of these books. They are also available on Amazon.com and other websites.

- Boutte, G. S. (2022). *Educating African American students*. Routledge.

- Boutte, G., Wynter-Hoyte, K., & Bryan, N. (2023). *Revolutionary love for early childhood classrooms: Nurturing the brilliance of young Black children*. Scholastic Incorporated.

- Boutte, G. S., Jackson, J. J., Collins, S. N., Baines, J. R., Broughton, A., & Johnson, G. L. (2024). *Pro-blackness in early childhood education: Diversifying curriculum and pedagogy in K-3 classrooms*. Teachers College Press.

- Johnson, L., Boutte, G. S., Greene, G., & Smith, D. (2018). *African Diaspora Literacy: The heart of transformation in K–12 schools and teacher education*. Lexington Books.

- King, J. E., & Swartz, E. E. (2014). *"Re-membering" history in student and teacher learning. An Afrocentric culturally informed praxis*. Routledge.

- Caldwell, K., & Chaves, E. (2020). *Engaging the African Diaspora in K–12 education*. Peter Lang.

- Lundy, B., & Negash, S. (20130. *Teaching Africa: A guide for the 21st-century classroom*. Indiana University Press.

Our fifth recommendation includes Black-owned book stores like the Brown Bookshelf. The Brown Bookshelf is an online resource of Black-centered children's, adolescent, and young adult books. We also include a link to a list of Black bookstores recommended by *Oprah Magazine*.

- The Brown Bookshelf: United in Story: https://the brownbookshelf.com/

- Mahogany Books: https://www.mahoganybooks.com

Other Black Bookstores

- *Oprah Magazine* list of Black bookstores: https://www. oprahmag.com/entertainment/book:s/a33497812/ black-owned-bookstores/

While we are providing resources, it is not an exhaustive list. There are thousands of credible resources available worldwide. Additionally, newer and more technologically advanced resources will be created after the publication of this book. However, we cannot ignore the history of poorly constructed and violent resources made about Black people around the Diaspora. Therefore, we warn readers not to use resources that present Black people using deficit lenses and perspectives. Find resources that present Black history through the lens and views of African-centered Black people. These resources can come from Black authors and illustrators and primary sources that focus on Black people's voices. While resources from white allies/co-conspirators (Love, 2019) are welcomed, it is crucial to gauge how they present information about Black people. Additionally, readers are advised to select resources about how African-descended people exhibited agency and joy in the face of endemic and systemic racism (King, 2019). Finally, remember that Blackness is global, and a complete Black history program is filled with knowledge and information from the entire Diaspora.

Stay well! We be lovin' you!

References

King, L. J. (Ed.). (2020). *Perspectives of Black histories in schools*. Information Age Publishing.

Love, B. L. (2019). *We want to do more than survive: Abolitionist teaching and the pursuit of educational freedom*. Beacon Press.

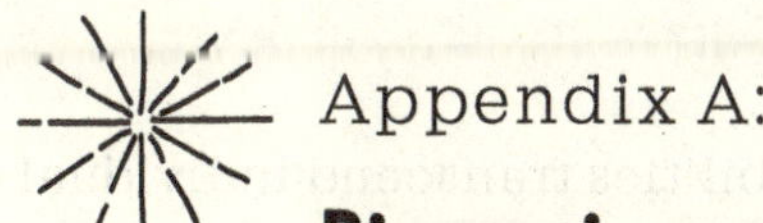

Appendix A:
Dimensions of African American Culture

1. **Oral tradition**—strengths in oral/aural modes of communication, in which both speaking and listening are treated as performances, and cultivation of oral virtuosity. The ability to use alliterative, metaphorically colorful, graphic forms of spoken language. This does not mean that strengths do not exist in written and other literacy traditions as well.

2. **Spirituality**—an approach to life as being essentially vitalistic rather than mechanistic, with the conviction that nonmaterial forces influence people's everyday lives

3. **Harmony**—the notion that one's fare is interrelated with other elements in the scheme of things, so that humankind and nature are harmonically conjoined

4. **Movement**—an emphasis on the interweaving of movement, rhythm, percussiveness, music, and dance, all of which are taken as central to psychological health

5. **Verve**—a propensity for relatively high levels of stimulation and for action that is energetic and lively

6. **Affect**—an emphasis on emotions and feelings, together with a specific sensitivity to emotional cues and a tendency to be emotionally expressive

7. **Communalism/collectivity**—a commitment to social connectedness, which includes an awareness that

social bonds and responsibilities transcend individual privilege

8. **Expressive individualism**—the cultivation of a distinctive personality and proclivity for spontaneous, genuine personal expression

9. **Social time perspective**—an orientation in which time is treated as passing through a social space rather than a material one, and in which time can be recurring, personal, and phenomenological

10. **Perseverance**—ability to maintain a sense of agency and strength in the face of adversities

11. **Improvisation**—substitution of alternatives that are more sensitive to Black culture. Examples can be seen in the artwork, music, language, clothing, food, and everyday culture.

Source: Boykin, 1994; Hale-Benson, 1986

References

Boykin, A. W. (1994). Afrocultural expression and its implications for schooling. In E.R. Hollins, J. E. King, & W.C. Hayman (Eds.), *Teaching diverse populations: Formulating a knowledge base* (pp. 243-273). State University of New York Press.

Hale-Benson, J. E. (1986). *Black children: Their roots, culture, and learning styles* (Rev. ed.). Johns Hopkins University Press.

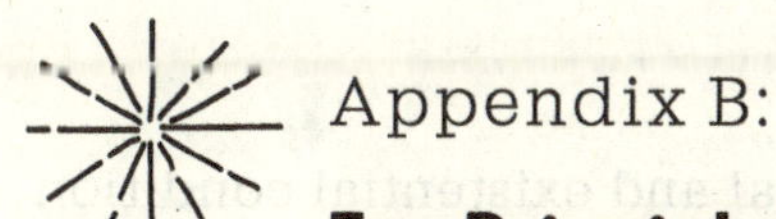

Appendix B:
Ten Principles for Black Education and Socialization

1. We exist as African People, an ethnic family. Our perspective must be centered in that reality.

2. The priority is on the African ethnic family over the individual. Because we live in a world where expertness in alien cultural traditions (that we also share) have gained hegemony, our collective survival and enhancement must be our highest priorities.

3. Some solutions to problems that involve differential use of three modes of response to domination and hegemony: Adaptation—adopting what is deemed useful; Improvisation—substituting or improvising alternatives that are more sensitive to our culture; and Resistance—resisting that which is destructive and not in the best interests of our people.

4. The "ways of knowing" provided by the arts and humanities are often more useful in informing our understanding of our lives and experiences and those of other oppressed people than the knowledge and methodologies of the sciences that have been privileged by the research establishment despite the often distorted or circumscribed knowledge and understanding this way of knowing produces.

5. Paradoxically, from the perspective of the education research establishment, knowledge production is viewed as the search for facts and (universal) truth, while the

circumstances of our social and existential condition require the search for meaning and understanding.

6. The priority is on research validity over inclusion. For research validity, highest priority must be placed on studies of:

   a) African tradition (history, culture, and language);

   b) Hegemony (e.g., uses of schooling/socialization and incarceration);

   c) Equity (funding, teacher quality, content, and access to technology); and

   d) Beneficial practice (at all levels of education, from childhood to elderhood).

7. Research informs practice and practice informs research in the production and utilization of knowledge; therefore, context is essential in research:

   a) cultural/historical context;

   b) political/ economic context; and

   c) professional context, including the history of AERA and African people.

8. We require power and influence over our common destiny. Rapid globalization of the economy and cyber-technology are transforming teaching, learning, and work itself. Therefore, we require access to education that serves our collective interests, including assessments that address

cultural excellence and a comprehensive approach to the interrelated health, learning, and economic needs of African people.

9. The Universal Declaration of Human Rights proclaims, and the UNESCO World Education 2000 Report, recently issued in Dakar, Senegal, affirms that "education is a fundamental human right" and "an indispensable means for effective participation in the societies and economies of the twenty-first century." We are morally obligated to "create safe, healthy, inclusive, and equitably resourced educational environments" conducive to excellence in learning and socialization with clearly defined levels of achievement for all. Such learning environments must include appropriate curricula and teachers who are appropriately educated and rewarded.

10. African people are not empty vessels. We are not new to the study of and practice of education and socialization that is rooted in deep thought. We will not accept a dependent status in the approach and solution to our problems.

Source: King, 2005

References

Hilliard, A. G. (1992). Behavioral style, culture, and teaching, and learning. *Journal of Negro Education, 61*(3), 370–377.

King, J. E. (2005). *Black education: A transformative research and action agenda for the new century*. Routledge.

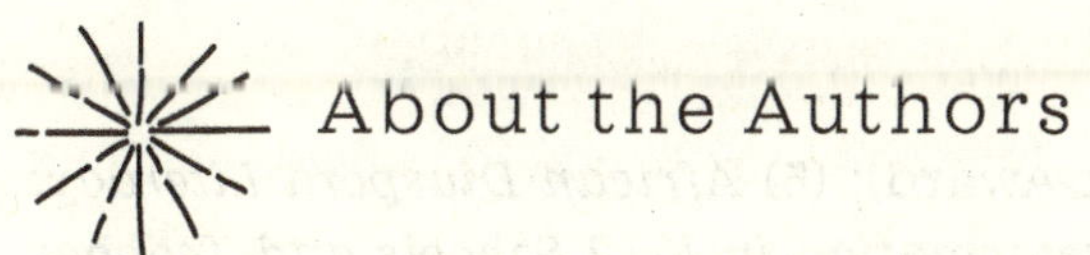

About the Authors

Janice Baines is a Clinical Instructor of Early Childhood Education at the University of South Carolina. She began her undergraduate studies at Benedict College, where she obtained a B.S. degree in early childhood education. She earned her M.Ed. in curriculum and instruction from the University of Wisconsin and is a Ph.D. student at the University of South Carolina. She is a co-author of *We've Been Doing it Your Way Long Enough: Choosing the Culturally Relevant Classroom* and *Pro-Blackness in Early Childhood Education: Diversifying Curriculum and Pedagogy in K-3 Classrooms*. Her research interests are Culturally Relevant and Sustaining Pedagogies, African Diaspora Literacy, and Black Feminist Thought.

Daphanie Bibbs is a doctoral scholar at the University at Buffalo. She is a Chicago native, lifelong learner, Black feminist, and facilitator of reformative conversations. Currently, Daphanie is a Graduate Fellow for the Center for K-12 Black History and Racial Literacy Education. Her research interests include how Black Mothers are policed in schools and the intersection of Black Girlhood and Black Motherhood.

Dr. Gloria Swindler Boutte is a Carolina Distinguished Professor at the University of South Carolina. She is the author/editor of eight books: (1) *Pro-Blackness in Early Childhood Education: Diversifying Curriculum and Pedagogy in K-3 Classrooms*; (2) *Revolutionary Love: Nurturing the Brilliance of Young Black Children*; (3) *Educating African American Students: And How Are the Children (2nd edition)*; (4) *We Be Lovin' Black Children: Becoming Learning to Be Literate About the African Diaspora* (2022 Society of Professors of Education

Outstanding Book Award); (5) *African Diaspora Literacy: The Heart of Transformation in K-12 Schools and Teacher Education* (2019 AESA Critics Choice Award); (6) *Educating African American Students: And How Are the Children*; (7) *Resounding Voices: School Experiences of People From Diverse Ethnic Backgrounds*; and (8) *Multicultural Education: Raising Consciousness*.

She has more than 100 publications and presents nationally and internationally. She has received prestigious awards such as the Fulbright Scholar; Fulbright Specialist; National Council of Teachers of English (NCTE) Outstanding Educator in the English Language Arts—Elementary Section; an AERA Division K Legacy Award; AERA 2022-23 Fellow Award; and an American Educational Research Association (AERA) Social Justice in Education Award. She was the founder and Executive Director of the Center for the Education and Equity of African American Students (CEEAAS). She has served as a Visiting Scholar and presented her work internationally on every continent except for Antarctica. She has led/co-led Fulbright Hays Groups projects in Ghana, Nigeria, Sierra Leone, Cameroon, and Barbados. She has been a Visiting Scholar in Australia (twice), South Africa, Jamaica, Guyana, and Colombia. She has traveled to nine countries in Africa (at least one country in each region) and lived in Nigeria for a year and taught at the University of Uyo as a Fulbright Scholar.

Dr. Boutte is the mother of three children and seven grandchildren—who typically travel with her.

Shayla Calhoun is an African American educator with more than 10 years of teaching experience. She has a Bachelor of Science in elementary education from the University of Southern Indiana and a Master of Arts from Oakland City University. She is currently working on obtaining a doctorate in educational leadership at the University of Southern Indiana. She brings to the table her own unique experiences along with a lifelong passion to empower students to be themselves and fully embrace it through literature.

Saudah N. Collins has served as an educator for 30 years and currently teaches in South Carolina. A former model teacher for the Center for the Education and Equity of African American Students (CEEAAS), she has dedicated her career to advancing equity in education. Saudah has taught pre-kindergarten through fifth grades and now specializes in African Studies. Saudah serves on the board of the South Carolina Council for Social Studies and has co-authored several professional publications. She has traveled to Cameroon, Ghana, Nigeria, and Barbados as a Fulbright-Hays participant and studied connections between Africa and the African Diaspora.

Saudah's achievements include the 2004 Presidential Award for Excellence in Mathematics and Science Teaching, recognition as the 2021 South Carolina History Teacher of the Year, and the National Council for the Social Studies Elementary Teacher of the Year. She also co-founded the International School of Educational Excellence in Bamenda, Cameroon.

Dr. Safi Darden is a senior lecturer in the Department of Psychology at the University of Exeter in the UK. Safi began her education in biology, ecology, and evolution and now carries out research in social behaviour and teaches and supervises undergraduate and graduate students majoring in both biology and psychology. She comes from a lineage of activists and critical, creative thinkers and intentionally focuses her service activities on creating equity of opportunity within her spheres of influence. She is co-founder of Black Heritage University Groups (B-HUGs), a collaborative project for social change driven by partnership and by community. After living outside the US for many years, for Safi, originally from New Jersey, contributing to this book has deep personal meaning.

Julia Dawson teaches sixth- and seventh-grade social studies at W. A. Perry Middle School in Columbia, South Carolina. She loves learning daily from W. A. Perry teenagers and their families; teachers, administrators, and staff; and local and state champions of education justice.

Jamon Dubose was born and raised in Aiken, South Carolina. He is a recent graduate of Aiken High School. He is attending college majoring in fine arts/education. Jamon is a local youth activist and leads a chapter of youth leaders called Next Generation. He frequently gives back to his community by volunteering.

Leslie K. Etienne is an Assistant Professor of Africana Studies and director of the Africana Studies program at Indiana University Indianapolis in the School of Liberal Arts. He is also the Founding Executive Director of the Center for Africana Studies and Culture and holds affiliate faculty appointments in American Studies and Museum Studies. Dr. Etienne's research interests are based at the intersections of Black Freedom Movement Histories, Cultural Heritage studies, Pan Africanism, and environmental justice and food sovereignty. His paramount research lies within the justice-based multigenerational emancipatory education found in the Student Nonviolent Coordinating Committee Freedom Schools enacted during the "Freedom Summer" in 1964. In the community, he is Executive Director for the IU Indianapolis Freedom School site. Committed to service both inside and outside of the university, he serves as the President of the Joseph Taylor Branch of the Association for the Study of African American Life and History.

Antoinette Gibson is a veteran Social Teacher in Richland One School District. Antoinette has received several rewards: Every Black Girl's Community Leader, #1 Scores for Standardized Testing in Social Studies, Best Early Bird Program in South Carolina, and WLTX Teacher of Week and recognition as a teacher for the Excellence and Equity of American Students. Antoinette has organized a boys' youth group to focus on academics and social and emotional well-being. She continues to mentor and motivate students to excel.

Valente' Gibson is an award-winning educator and leader with a passion for equity, literacy, and student engagement. He is currently the Assistant Principal at Jackson Creek Elementary in Richland School District Two, where he previously taught third and fifth grade and was named both school and district Teacher of the Year. A published author and national presenter, Gibson has been recognized by the International Literacy Association as a "Top 30 Under 30" and a SCALE (South Carolina Afterschool Leaders Empowered) fellow. He continues to champion student-centered excellence through critical instructional practices and a commitment to student achievement.

Abigail Henry is a Schomburg Fellow and doctoral student at University at Buffalo. As a graduate fellow at UB's K-12 Teaching Black History and Racial Center, she serves as the instructor for the Teaching Black History micro-credential program. Prior to moving to Buffalo, Abigail taught ninth grade African American History at a charter school in west Philadelphia for twelve years. In Philadelphia, she spearheaded development of the African American History curriculum through curricula writing and professional development.

Dr. Kayla Hostetler has been an educator for sixteen years. She holds a Ph.D. in Language and Literacy from the University of South Carolina, where her dissertation, *The Tale of Two Pandemics*, explored how culturally sustaining pedagogy can be effectively implemented within blended learning spaces. Her research argues that culturally sustaining and anti-racist pedagogies can be successfully carried out across both digital and physical classrooms, ensuring that student identity, equity, and voice remain central to learning.

Dr. Hostetler is an accomplished scholar and practitioner who has published widely on topics related to literacy, pedagogy, and social justice. Her publications include work in *English Leadership Quarterly*, *The Clearing House*, and *The Bread Loaf Teacher Network Journal*, as well as chapters in edited collections on equity and literacy education. She consistently presents at state, national, and international conferences, speaking on subjects such as rewriting dominant narratives, centering student voice and advocacy, examining positionality and privilege, equitable representation in curriculum, the pedagogy of play, and culturally sustaining teaching practices.

Her influence extends beyond the classroom into leadership and mentorship. As an Education Specialist with Write to Change and a mentor with the Next Generation Youth Leadership Network, Dr. Hostetler works with students to help them discover their voices, take steps toward social action, and see themselves as agents of change. She views teaching as a form of activism, rooted in the belief that education must be both transformative and restorative.

At the heart of Dr. Hostetler's practice is the philosophy of *educational love*. She believes that love in education is not abstract but active, it is the work of affirming all students as worthy of dignity and respect, seeking justice alongside them, and guiding them into difficult but necessary conversations about truth, identity, and equity. For her, educational love means empowering student voices, cultivating critical thinking, and preparing young people to imagine and build a more just world.

Outside of her professional work, Dr. Hostetler loves reading literature, traveling, writing, and spending time with her two daughters.

Dr. Joy Howard earned her Ph.D. in Educational Foundations at the University of South Carolina where she met and learned from her teacher, Dr. Gloria Boutte. She has held several academic positions across the United States. She is now an Associate Professor in the Leadership and Educational Studies Department at Appalachian State University where she works with students in the Ed.D. program in Educational Leadership. Her work focuses on leadership for constructing humanizing educational communities. She is especially interested in humanizing spacemaking and community engaged leadership within a racist society. She is the author of over thirty published articles and a co-editor of a recent book, *All-in: Community Engaged Research* published with Myers Press. As a leader with the URBAN action research network, Joy is interested in how to work in and with communities to create positive change. As a motherscholar she has co-presented and co-published work with her sons relative to their interests and first-hand accounts relative to Black mixed race youth experiences in schools.

Dr. Jarvais J. Jackson is a former elementary teacher and current Assistant Professor of Elementary Literacy Education at Indiana University Indianapolis. His work is grounded in pro-Blackness, culturally sustaining pedagogy, and the educational wellness of Black students and teachers. Drawing on qualitative and community-based research, Dr. Jackson partners with schools and families to prepare educators who center Black children's lived experiences and affirm their brilliance. His scholarship explores family engagement, African Diaspora Literacy, and school-university partnerships that move beyond transactional involvement toward shared power and co-creation.

As a scholar-practitioner, Dr. Jackson actively collaborates and publishes with classroom teachers as part of his research, ensuring their voices remain central in efforts to transform education. Before joining IUI, he served as a Program Director and Assistant Professor at Georgia Southern University, where he led innovative teacher preparation efforts and built strong partnerships with local schools. He also directed statewide equity-focused initiatives through the Center for the Education and Equity of African American Students (CEEAAS).

Dr. Jackson currently serves on the Board of Directors for the National Association for School-University Partnerships (NASUP). His work has been published by Teachers College Press, and in *The Urban Review* and *The Reading Teacher*, and presented at AERA, NCTE, and the Black Doctoral Network. Across his teaching, research, and service, he remains committed to sustaining liberatory educational spaces where Black children and their communities can thrive.

Dr. Tambra O. Jackson is the Dean of the School of Education at Indiana University Indianapolis and Professor of Urban Teacher Education. She is also an affiliate faculty in the Africana Studies program. Dr. Jackson considers herself a scholar-activist and is committed to social justice issues pertaining to the historical and contemporary oppression, miseducation, and liberation of children of color in U.S. schools. Dr. Jackson has contributed nationally and locally to the Children's Defense Fund Freedom Schools. Her research on Freedom Schools is pioneering in the field of teacher education. She has published on how teacher education can learn from and build upon the work of the CDF Freedom Schools model for teacher learning and the ways in which the program offers a liberatory space for children of color. She has established and led Freedom School sites in 3 states—Michigan, South Carolina, and Indiana. Dr. Jackson has authored over 40 scholarly publications and is the editor of the book, *Black Mother Educators: Advancing Praxis for Access, Equity and Achievement* (2021). She is a committed partner to her husband, Leslie, and the proud mother of a genius fourth grader, Kadir.

Dawnavyn James is a former early childhood, elementary, and Black history educator. She is the author of *Beyond February: Teaching Black History Any Day, Every Day, and All Year Long* and researches early childhood and elementary Black history learning, instruction, and curriculum development through the history of Black education and Black women educators. Dawnavyn is a doctoral student at the University at Buffalo.

Dr. George L. Johnson is Professor and Academic Program Coordinator of Special Education at South Carolina State University. For more than two decades, Dr. Johnson's scholarship, teaching, and service has focused on equity pedagogies, teaching for social justice, and critical race theory in education with an emphasis on culturally and linguistically diverse students. He has taught and presented nationally and internationally on special education, diversity, and disproportionality, community, and equity issues. Dr. Johnson has numerous publications and has received $300,000 in grants. He has presented his work in Nigeria, Australia, New Zealand, England, Botswana, South Africa, and Sierra Leone. He is the co-author (with Gloria Boutte) of *Drs. Diaspora* Curriculum-a curriculum that teaches P-12 students about African and African American history.

Dr. Lasana D. Kazembe is an Emmy Award-winning poet, educator, and critical Black scholar whose work examines culture, race, history, the arts, and the social context of education. His research, teaching, activism, and creative scholarship comprise a philopraxis that explores the rich and sentient 'lost-found' sacred epistemologies (i.e., history, expressive forms, imaginaries, folklore, futurities) of Africana peoples and situates them as sites of memory, critical pedagogy, cultural production, and social action. Dr. Kazembe's related interests include history and historiography, the cultural foundations of art and artmaking, intellectual and mass culture, Black radical thought and transnational social movements, the politics of art and art criticism, and the genesis and genealogy of Global Black Arts Movements and the Black Intellectual Tradition. He is the recipient of multiple teaching awards including the Indiana University Trustees Teaching Award, Burton W. Gorman Teaching Award, and the Chancellor's Award for Excellence in Multicultural Teaching. His writings on education, race, and culture have appeared in numerous peer-reviewed scholarly journals including *The Journal of Black Studies, International Journal of Qualitative Studies in Education,* and *Race, Ethnicity and Education.* Dr. Kazembe serves as faculty in the IU Indianapolis School of Education and the IU Indy Africana Studies Program. He also serves as Associate Director of the IU Indianapolis Arts & Humanities Institute and sits on the Executive Advisory Committee for the Center for Africana Studies and Culture.

Dr. Joyce E. King holds the Benjamin E. Mays Endowed Chair for Urban Teaching, Learning and Leadership at Georgia State University (GSU) in the Department of Educational Policy Studies. She holds affiliated faculty status in the Department of African American Studies, the Women's and Gender Studies Institute, the Partnership for Urban Health Research, and the Urban Studies Institute. Her publications in the *Harvard Educational Review,* the *Journal of Negro Education, International Journal of Qualitative Studies in Education,* and the *Journal of African American History* focus on a transformative role for culture in curriculum and urban teacher effectiveness, morally engaged, community-mediated inquiry and Black education research and policy. Her most recent book is *Heritage Knowledge in the Curriculum: Retrieving an African Episteme* (with E. Swartz). Dr. King is past president of the American Educational Research Association, President of the Board of Directors of the Institute for Food and Development Policy (FoodFirst.org), a member of the National African American Reparations Commission and a recipient of the Stanford University School of Education Alumni Excellence Award (2018). A recent essay, "To Create a More Perfect Union, We the People Need Reparations to Heal Our Wounded Souls," is published on the American Civil Liberties Union website: https://www.aclu.org/issues/create more-perfect-union-we-people-need-reparations-heal-our wounded-souls

Dr. LaGarrett J. King is a Professor and Founding Director for the Center for K-12 Black History and Racial Literacy Education at the University at Buffalo. With over 60 publications, Dr. King is a sought after speaker and leader in Black history education. He is a former classroom teacher who researches the teaching and learning of Black history in schools and society, teacher education and professional development, and the history of Black education.

Preston King is a freshman student athlete in New York state. He helped establish the first middle school Black student union in his school district and served as the first president. His goal is to earn a football scholarship after high school and become an entrepreneur afterwards.

Dr. Melody Kuziwa Jombe is a Zimbabwean academic, strategic management lecturer, and Deputy Programme Director (Business School: WYA with Year Abroad) at the University of Exeter Business School. She brings to academia a wealth of experience from the corporate sector, having previously worked across Fast-Moving Consumer Goods (FMCG) and market research industries. Her doctoral research utilised a critical incident technique to explore the causal attributions of venture distress, reflecting her continued interest in resilience, agency, and decision-making in uncertain environments.

Before joining Exeter, Melody contributed as an academic reviewer for Southern New Hampshire University's GEM Hub initiative, which expands access to higher education for vulnerable and under-resourced learners across global contexts.

In 2024, she co-founded the Black Heritage University Groups (B-HUGs) in collaboration with schools within the Ted Wragg Trust. Rooted in principles of Black consciousness, visibility, and representation, B-HUGs provides mentoring, role modelling, and campus immersion experiences for Black high school students in Exeter. The initiative directly responds to the underrepresentation of Black academics within UK higher education and seeks to cultivate belonging and aspiration within spaces historically closed to students of African and Afro-Diasporic heritage.

Melody's work is driven by a commitment to widening participation, reimagining access, and ensuring that the next generation of Black scholars and leaders are not only welcomed into higher education—but recognised, empowered, and seen.

Dr. Clement T. M. Lambert is Chair of the Department of Teaching and Learning at Northern Arizona University, where he leads initiatives in literacy education, teacher preparation, and inclusive pedagogy. His academic journey began in Jamaica, where he served as Senior Lecturer and Program Coordinator at the University of the West Indies, overseeing literacy studies across undergraduate and graduate programs and managing the Joint Board of Teacher Education.

Dr. Lambert's scholarship centers on literacy education, with a more recent focus on African Diaspora Literacy and African Indigenous Knowledge. His work in this area bridges theory and practice, contributing to culturally responsive teaching and curriculum development. Over the years, Dr. Lambert has conducted research, published extensively, and led national and international projects aimed at literacy development, teacher education, and violence prevention in schools. He has consulted on initiatives supported by UNESCO, UNICEF, USAID, and Jamaica's Ministry of Education, helping shape national strategies for literacy improvement and preparing pre-service teachers to become literacy specialists.

International collaboration is a hallmark of his career. Dr. Lambert has presented at global conferences—including as a keynote speaker for the International Reading Association—and served on editorial search committees for leading journals such as the *Journal of Adolescent and Adult Literacy*. His public service includes leadership roles with the Jamaica Library Service Board and the Literacy Assessment and Monitoring Program (LAMP).

He holds a Doctorate in Elementary Education from the University of Alberta. Dr. Lambert continues to mentor students from undergraduate to doctoral levels and remains deeply committed to fostering literacy leadership, inclusive pedagogies, and educational transformation.

Shaquetta Moultrie is a middle-level social studies teacher. She has scored number one in standardized testing for African American males. She was honored as Law Educator of the Year for the South Carolina Bar association for her work with middle-level mock trial students.

Dr. Asangha Ngufor Muki is a university lecturer of psychology and at the same time a researcher at the University of Bamenda, Northwest Region of Cameroon. His areas of interest in terms of research are in child/adolescent development, peer relationship, and youth culture in relationship to the development of resilience. He is equally an African cultural constructivist as well as a strong advocate of African Indigenous Knowledge Systems (AIKS) and its role in the development of Africa. He is affiliated to the Center for Research on Child and Family Development and Education (CRCFDE), Limbe, Cameroon and he is active in several national and international bodies. Currently he is a member of Cameroon Psychology Association (CPA), International Society for the Study of Behavioural Development (ISSBD), International Association of Cross Cultural Psychology (IACCP), and Center for the Education and Equity of African American Students (CEEAAS) at USC. He was a lecturer for the 2017 Fulbright Hays Groups Abroad project in Cameroon.

Rabbi Dr. Meir Muller is the Associate Dean of Community Empowerment at the College of Education, University of South Carolina. His research focuses on advancing Pro-Blackness and Pro-Jewishness in education, fostering Black–Jewish solidarity, combating antisemitism, promoting anti-racist pedagogies, and strengthening early childhood education. He played a key role in developing South Carolina's early childhood state standards, co-edited *Early Childhood Jewish Education: Multicultural, Gender, and Constructivist Perspectives*, and co-founded and led the Cutler Jewish Day School for 30 years.

Dr. Kindel Turner Nash is the Spangler Distinguished Professor of Early Child Literacy in the Reich College of Education's Department of Child Development, Literacy, and Special Education at Appalachian State University. She received her Ph.D. from the University of South Carolina in 2012. Turner Nash's research, teaching, and service centers on culturally sustaining and humanizing early literacy practices, highly effective teachers, and transformative approaches to teacher preparation. Her classroom-based research has resulted in the co-development of a complex reading model, the Cultural Sustenance View of Reading, and the co-authorship of three books and 35 refereed publications. The book *Culturally Sustaining Practices for PreK-3rd*

Classrooms: The Children Come Full, co-authored with class-room teachers, was recently recognized as an Edward Fry Book Award finalist by the Literacy Research Association (2023). Nash has received hundreds of thousands of dollars in grants from numerous sources, including the U.S. Department of Education and the Spencer Foundation. In 2022, Turner Nash was named the Early Literacy Teacher Educator of the Year by the National Council of Teachers of English.

Ricardo O. Neal is the President & Chief Executive Officer of We Will All Rise, or "All Rise." He guides the organization's decision-making, strategy development, fundraising, and fiscal management in this role. He leads the organization's work in creating targeted initiatives that invest in the social and academic trajectories of young men of color. Over the past 25 years, Ricardo served in various leadership and governance roles within the education, philanthropy, and public advocacy sectors and has led community change work nationally and internationally. Ricardo earned a Bachelor's degree in Political Science from the University of Massachusetts, Amherst, and a Master's degree in Social Work from the Boston University School of Social Work. Ricardo has helped cities and school districts develop programs and strategies to improve students' and families' life outcomes in high-need communities. Born in St. Catherine, Jamaica, and raised in Lawrence, Massachusetts, Ricardo lives in Baltimore, MD, with his wife and two children.

Dr. Samuel Ntewusu is the Director of the Institute of African Studies at the University of Ghana. He teaches Chieftaincy and Development in Africa (undergraduate course) and, in collaboration with other lecturers, teaches the following postgraduate courses: The Slave Trade and Africa, African Historiography and Methodology, Colonial Rule and African Responses, and Pan Africanism. He has supervised a number of graduate students in their research projects/theses both in and outside of Ghana. He has presented internationally in Europe and the U.S. He has hosted numerous Fulbright-Hays Groups Abroad projects and other academic delegations in Ghana.

Dr. Moepeola Omoegun is Vice Chancellor at Monarch University in Nigeria. She has taught as a Professor of Guidance and Counseling at the University of Lagos (UNILAG), Nigeria. Dr. Omoegun served as a former Dean of the Faculty of Education UNILAG and Pioneer Dean of Education for Ajayi Crowther University, Oyo. She is also a member of the Governing Council of Ajayi Crowther University, Oyo. In 2018, she hosted a Fulbright Hays Groups Abroad project in Nigeria.

Ayanna Page is a Pastoral Support Advisor and Equality, Diversity and Inclusion (EDI) Assistant at a Secondary School in Devon, England. Ayanna's role bridges both pastoral and inclusion work, supporting students through mentoring, advocacy, and everyday conversations that nurture confidence, identity, and self-belief. She works closely with staff to raise awareness of issues surrounding discrimination, identity, and equality, ensuring that student voice and wellbeing remain at the heart of school culture.

Of mixed heritage, with family roots in Trinidad & Tobago and the UK, Ayanna brings her lived experience to her advocacy for inclusion and anti-racism in education. Her work is centred on ensuring that all students feel seen, heard, and valued, especially those who may not always see themselves reflected in their school environment.

Through her partnership with B-HUGs, Ayanna has witnessed the power of representation and community in helping young people embrace their heritage with pride. The programme has been transformative not only for her students but also for her personally, reaffirming her belief in the power of education to create lasting change. Ayanna is proud to build belonging every day, helping students believe in themselves and see the beauty in who they are.

Dr. Gregory Simmons received his Ph.D. from the University at Buffalo in 2025. Currently, he is a teacher and curriculum specialist at the American School of Benguerir in Morrocco. His research focuses on the teaching and learning of Black history education, white teachers, and whiteness studies in education.

Dr. Nicole Yvette Strange-Martin is a Professor of Reading and Literacy Studies and an administrator at Alabama State University. She previously served as dean at Trinity Washington University and Claflin University. A passionate educator, she focuses on the educational experiences of first-generation minority students and evidence-based teaching practices. She has received Faculty Excellence Awards in both Research and Teaching.

Dr. Strange-Martin authored *Essentials of Reading: Strategies and Practice for High School and College Readers*, with two additional textbooks in press. Her scholarly work includes peer-reviewed publications and national and international presentations. She has traveled to over 20 countries to develop partnerships, present at conferences, and share literacy practices—including service in China and the Bahamas through the People to People Ambassador Program.

She also presented at the Oxford University Roundtable in England. Beyond her academic work, she is a mother, wife, mentor, artist, and colleague.

Wahida Sussex, a British Bangladeshi educator, moved from a large, diverse city to a small village in Exeter, Devon, over a decade ago. Entering the education sector five years ago, she quickly noticed the underrepresentation of ethnic minorities within schools and voiced this during her interview, not as a criticism, but as a call to action. Drawing on her lived experience of inner-city life, cultural diversity, and resilience, she brings a rich and meaningful perspective to her work with young people.

Wahida began her journey at St James School as a Teaching Assistant, where her one-to-one work with students with SEND allowed her to build deep knowledge and empathy for individual needs. Her skill set and confidence quickly grew, leading her to take the initiative in developing and managing the school's sensory room—a calm, inclusive space that supports students' emotional regulation, well-being, and sense of safety. This work, combined with her strong organisational and interpersonal abilities, led her into her current role as Assistant SENDCo.

She is also the co-founder of the B-HUGs brand—a name with dual meaning: *Black Hugs*, symbolising warmth, care, and community, and *Black Heritage University Group*, celebrating identity, culture, and belonging. B-HUGs began as an idea but evolved into a powerful weekly programme, enriching the lives of students at St James, particularly during the summer term. Its focus on empowerment, mentorship, and cultural pride has supported countless students as the school's "upcoming kings and queens" and given them a space where they feel seen and celebrated.

Wahida's passion lies in championing equality, diversity, and inclusion in every aspect of school life. Through B-HUGs and her broader SEND work, she is a visible and trusted role model for students from all backgrounds. Her leadership ensures that all young people at St James feel represented, supported, and equipped to thrive. Honoured to be a part of this book as it has healed so many parts of life and I cannot wait for what the future holds for B-HUGs!

Dr. Berte Van Wyk is a former chairperson of the Caribbean and African Studies in Education Special Interest Group at the American Educational Research Association. He is the current president of the African Development and Education Research Association. He is also a former chairperson of the Department of Education Policy Studies at Stellenbosch University in South Africa. His research focuses on institutional culture, Indigenous Khoikhoi and San epistemologies, and philosophy of higher education.

Jaliyah S. Ware is a sophomore at South University and is studying to be a neonatal care nurse. She is an Africanist, with her first visit to the continent (Kenya) when she was seven. One of her favorite places is Ghana, having gone three times so far. Jaliyah is an excellent writer and hair stylist as well. She was a member of the founding girls' group, *Drs. Diaspora*. She attended 'Dear School' (her grandmother's name for Black history lessons) from ages three to 14.

Janiyah S. Ware is a sophomore at Denmark Technical College, majoring in barbering and culinary arts. She has visited Kenya and Ghana, having gone three times so far. Janiyah is an excellent writer and budding chef. She was a member of the founding girls group, *Drs. Diaspora*. She attended 'Dear School' (her grandmother's name for Black history lessons) from ages three to 14.

Dr. Kamania Wynter-Hoyte is an Associate Professor in the Department of Instruction of Teacher Education at University of South Carolina. Her academic pursuits are deeply rooted in African Diaspora Literacies, with a particular focus on fostering liberation within teacher education and early childhood environments. She has co-authored two impactful books: *Revolutionary Love for Early Childhood Classrooms: Nurturing the Brilliance of Young Black Children* and *Revolutionary Love: Creating a Culturally Inclusive Literacy Classroom*. She also has scholarly articles published in prestigious academic journals, including *Language Arts, International Critical*

Childhood Policy Studies Journal, Journal of Negro Education, Journal of Literacy Research, and *International Journal of Qualitative Studies in Education*. Her commitment to excellence and innovation has been recognized with the 2018 Early Childhood Assembly's Early Literacy Educator of the Year Award from the National Council Teachers of English.